SAMBOLI! Beware!

LAKSHMAN

Translated from Kannada by
SUSHEELA PUNITHA

THORNBIRD
NIYOGI BOOKS

Published by
NIYOGI BOOKS
Block D, Building No. 77,
Okhla Industrial Area, Phase-I,
New Delhi-110 020, INDIA
Tel: 91-11-26816301, 26818960
Email: niyogibooks@gmail.com
Website: www.niyogibooksindia.com

Design: Shashi Bhushan Prasad
Cover Illustration: Arun Kumar G.

ISBN: 978-93-86906-35-9
Publication: 2018

Printed at: Niyogi Offset Pvt. Ltd., New Delhi, India

Contents

Remembering Father

Father died on 1 November 2017 while the proofs of this work were being checked. After dinner, he complained of uneasiness in the chest, and he slipped away before we could take him to hospital.

It is impossible and even pointless to talk or write about Father merely by stringing words together. It is our good fortune that we were born as his children. And we hope to live as he lived. His life was exemplary.

A father or a teacher or an elder scolds or beats children to train them. But Father never beat us, never scolded us. He trained us with his silence and by example. He was soft-spoken and gentle, a man of few words. He was humane in his dealings. But his family was not his only concern. He believed he was called for a purpose, and he lived and worked for this purpose with an inner courage and determination even when he could see that his efforts were not always worthwhile. He took on the struggle for the betterment of the exploited among the outcastes and became one of the guiding spirits of regional and national movements to fight discrimination based on caste. His vision was a casteless society. He was larger than life. He was named Lachmaiah by his parents, but he was called Lakshmanji by people who looked upon him as their leader. More than all this, he showed us how to live with self-worth, rising beyond differences of caste or class. He is our inspiration and our guiding spirit.

Whatever be the problems in our family, whatever be our problems that we brought to him as children, he laughed. That was his first reaction, that soft laughter. And then he would sort it out slowly, patiently. He never seemed upset or scared. We got to understand his ways as we grew older. We also learnt that that was the only right way of doing things.

Father never held me, or my elder brother Gowtham, or my younger sister Samathavani by the hand to take us to school like other fathers. He never played with us. He never took us out anywhere. I hardly remember a time when we went out together on a family-outing. He kept all his time to work for the betterment of the lower castes and the untouchables to relieve them of their pain, their disgrace; the pain of disgrace that he had endured. He was always preoccupied with finding ways out of the differential treatment meted out towards people considered lower by birth.

Father had a way of staring at us silently at times. The love in his eyes at such times made us happy and we wished and watched out for that stare. As a husband and a father, he knew what we needed and what we did not and provided for us at the right time, even without us asking. We did not have to stretch out our hands to anyone else.

Our parents were not like other husbands and wives. The caring and friendship between them was amazing; they were so compatible, so similar. The rare moments when they sat together, chatting and laughing, were precious to us. I guess each of those was precious to Amma too; she would refer to it the whole day and laugh over it with us. On his last day, the first of November, Prof. Susheela Punitha had called him up in the morning to consult him about the cover-page design for her translation of his athma-kathe *Samboli!*. That made him very happy. He told Amma his athma-kathe would be out in English by early next year; it would be prescribed in colleges, and students would get to read it and learn to be humane and to stand up for justice. Amma laughed that Father always dreamed big. But that was who he was, as an activist and as a writer. We have kept his room as he left it, with his files and his pen and his glasses where he left them, intending to return.

There were rarer occasions when he talked to us too, say for ten or fifteen minutes at the most. But they were filled with his love for us, his hope for us, his belief in us. I would hanker for such conversation every time he was at home and not be preoccupied with worries larger than our lives. At such times, I glimpsed the meaning of the saying 'Speech is silver but silence is golden'. But today I know that my father is beyond comparison. He was the most precious person in the world to me.

Jaibheem

9 December 2017, Bengaluru

Author's Note

Ever since I can remember, I have been asking, 'Why? Why?' At school, my teacher in the third class was a Brahmin with a vertical naama caste-mark on his forehead, black cap and coat and a kacche-panche, that formal way of wearing the panche, drawing the edge between the legs and tucking it in at the back at the waist. He made the Vokkaliga children sit in the front rows and us, Madigas in the back rows a little beyond them. He had two canes, one was the regular size, measuring from the elbow to the tip of his middle finger, but the other was as long as a baaru, measuring from the tip of the middle finger of one hand to the tip of the middle finger of the other with both arms outstretched. He used the short one to punish the Vokkaligas and the long one to beat us, flicking it with his arm outstretched, stinging us wherever it landed, whipping off a bit of flesh. Why this difference in punishment that left us scarred with stripes? He once beat me without warning. I winced. After class, he told me that he had seen me touch his bicycle. What was wrong with that?

At home, the members of the master's family cared for our well-being, and yet, why did they and even their children address my parents and grandparents disrespectfully? Why did they serve us on castor leaves in the cowshed with its perpetual stench of dung and urine? It was not just them. During Sri Rama Navami celebrations, panaka was served to passers-by in leaf cups to quench their thirst. But when *we* went for a drink, we had to hold our cupped hands to our mouths and it would be poured from such a height that most of it squirted out wetting our clothes. One's tongue would get perhaps a drop or two to taste the delicious sweetness of jaggery in lime juice.

I realized only much later that the difference in treatment had nothing to do with what we did or did not do. It had nothing to do with whether people were good to us or not. It had to do with the age-old caste system that cheated our people of their basic right to human dignity. Our people had mouths, true, but no voice to voice their plight because they had no education. I barely completed my high school. I have been writing poems and stories since 1989. I began my athma-kathana when I was forty and took fifteen years to finish it. *Samboli!* traces my growth from my awareness that I was not seen as a person but as a Madiga to my awareness that as a Madiga, I am a man with a mission.

I had barely sprouted a moustache when my friend V Basavaraju called me to be an activist. I participated in a torchlight protest rally organized by the Dalit Sangarsha Samiti in 1979 in Binnypete, Bengaluru, protesting the death of a Holeya at the hands of a Gowda because he did not remove the carcass of a cow from the village. Now I could see myself as a part of a larger persona, the Samiti; I had found a community identity.

Samboli! is the life story of the movement as well. Here, I found my voice as a member of an association that resisted the injustices of discrimination meted out to the Holeyas and

Madigas based on caste prejudice. The Samiti was the forum that moulded me into a social activist to claim basic human dignity for the lower castes. I developed a moral conviction that we were fighting to redress a wrong, even when we were not always successful in our campaigns. Even when we learnt the hard way that power and money have insidious ways of stifling our cause, we carried on regardless in the belief that fight we must without counting the cost.

But I parted ways from the Samiti when it compromised its commitment to the common good of all Dalits and began to favour one sect at the expense of another to serve the self-interest of its members; and when social activism took on a political dimension and activists pawned the interests of the community to gain positions of power.

When I lost faith in the Samiti, I found my voice as a writer to continue my strife.

Samboli! means echcharike in Kannada—'*Be careful!*'

Samboli! This expression is not from yesterday or the day before; it is centuries old.

Manu, the ancient lawgiver, decreed that people belonging to any of the untouchable castes of this country had to hold a pole with jingling bells tied to one end and pound it on the ground at every step to make a sound—jal-jal. They had to call out, '*Samboli! Samboli*!' This is the Samboli pole warning others of their presence. They were to walk only on conservancy lanes and not on the main streets and only around noon when their shadow was tucked under their feet and would not pollute people of the upper castes by falling on them.

Samboli!, by extension, could imply '*Beware!*' in the present context of Dalit uprisings. It could also be a clarion call for Dalits to fight for their humanity.

I was born on 3 May 1957 in Kathriguppe village, south Bangalore. My father Muthappa and mother Venkatamma were daily-wage labourers. I walked to the Government Primary School in the village and the Government Boys Middle School, Basavanagudi before moving to Sri Narasimharaja Hostel, Chamrajapet to do my high school at Old Fort High School, Chamarajapet. From 1980, I have been a second-division clerk at Sree Veerendra Patil Pre-university College of Arts, Science and Commerce run by the Hyderabad Karnataka Education Society. In 1985, I founded Pragathi Education Society that runs the Pragathi Degree College for Dalit students.

From 1992, I was one of the founder members of the Karnataka Vimochana Ranga with other social activists and served as Joint-Secretary until 2000. Since then, I have been the founder member of Jaathi Vinaasha Vedike that fights for our constitutional right to equality at the national level. Our activities have to be social only; never political.

I look forward to a casteless society. I desire that my writings will be a refrain to the voiceless dirge of my people. I hold my struggle and my writing as the very breath of my being through which I fight with the hope that social inequalities may cease; that equality may reign. It is my one desire that we talk to one another with open minds and laugh with one another with open hearts.

I cannot express my happiness when Susheelamma Punitha called me one day and said, 'I would like to translate your athma-kathe into English.' To translate a piece of writing dealing with sensitive issues is indeed a difficult task. Not just that; it is not easy to grasp, still less translate, the local variety of Kannada used by our Madiga community. I remember the time I stretched out my arms while telling her that the cane used to punish us in school was as long as a baaru and she said she knew that unit of length as a maaru; flower-vendors stretched out their arms similarly to measure strands of jasmine. I know she has painstakingly understood and transcreated the language of abuse, protests, fights, food habits and cultural practices in *Samboli*! She asked if she could add an exclamation point to the title. It is an excellent idea. *Samboli!* conveys our excitement in what we have accomplished and our hope in what we wish to achieve. *Samboli!* has gained a meaning it did not have when my ancestors used it. My boundless thanks to Susheelamma Punitha.

My grateful thanks to Shrimathi Mini Krishnan too. Her help and encouragement have been a unique experience for me. As per her suggestion, I have added an afterword to my athma-kathana.

Lakshman
Translated by Susheela Punitha

Translator's Note

We shall not cease from exploration.
The end of all exploring
Will be to arrive where we started
And know the place for the first time.

T S Eliot, 'Little Gidding',
the last of the *Four Quartets*

That is how I felt when I read Lakshman's *Samboli!* I had to begin at the very beginning, for I was ill-equipped to translate his athma-kathe, despite what I had learnt as a hands-on translator.

The structure of the text is anecdotal and the style is in the variety that his people speak; it is densely referential, taking the contextual references for granted. How could I translate the flavour of the context from which the text gains its signification when I did not even know what some of the expressions implied? The allusions to some experiences in Lakshman's childhood are unintelligible, if translated literally. They needed to be elaborated to make sense. I asked him to explain the terms to me. He did and it helped. For instance, he writes about the people at the Banavara village fair who fascinated him as a child; people who entertain at the fair to earn a few rupees. A literal translation of the passage would read: *'There were those who played with gangetthu…And there were men from the Muslim tribes who did the kankattu.'* But such a transliteration does not ensure the impact of the original in the translation. And so, I had to elaborate the two expressions and transcreate the passage as: *There were those who played with gangetthu. They paraded a decorated bull, cow and calf around the fair as Rama, Sita and Lakshmana. They asked Rama, the bull, "Will you marry Sita, Rama?" The bull would nod in response to a stealthy tug from his master and one of them would collect donations for the wedding. And then there were the men from the Muslim tribes who did the kankattu. These were acts of mesmerizing the audience, based on faith, not reason. Calling upon the power of Allah, some split granite slabs into two neat pieces with a bare hand; three men writhed out together through an impossibly small loop…and went among the spectators begging for alms in the name of Allah the Powerful.* This is translation, as I understand it. It not only brings out the meaning of the two expressions, but also transfers the ambience and flavour of the Kannada context to enhance its reach in the English text.

But, could I interpolate such a long passage into the text? True, I had heard it from the writer himself, but would I be exploiting the sanctity of the written text?

And then I saw.

Samboli! is not only an athma-kathe. It is an allegory. But it is not a pilgrim's linear progress towards personal salvation. *Samboli!* is the life story of a man and his movement. It is an account of his efforts to redeem his self-worth by redeeming the self-worth of his people. And his journey is not yet over, for his vision includes an eschatological dimension in which each one of us has a part to play. Lakshman closes his Author's Note with, '*It is my one desire that we talk to one another with open minds and laugh with one another with open hearts.*' This hope recalls the Banavara santhe as an image of a community where people with different religious convictions but with a shared culture come together in fellowship to have fun and to earn a living. Lakshman's journey has taken a circuitous route, but he plods on with the conviction that he is the voice of the voiceless and the hope that his desire will be fulfilled someday.

Now I could justify the interpolation. It is not an intrusion, since the scaffolding becomes more organic than structural. It focuses more on the flavour than the meaning which could have been provided with footnotes, though they would have stalled the flow of the narrative. The image reinforces the theme of lost and hope-to-find, as Lakshman, in his search for his identity, realizes he is set apart for a purpose. The expression athma-kathana describes *Samboli!* as the story of his spirit, for it traces the growth of Lakshman's awareness that he is not seen as a person but as a Madiga, the lowest of the low castes in Karnataka, to his awareness that as a Madiga, he is a man with a mission. Interpolations such as this oral rendering provide an immediate insight into the richness of the writer's experience. As a visual image it becomes deeply metaphorical, offering multiple interpretations of the amity of community life without taking sides. The orality of the narrative is also retained through proverbs and songs, since Lakshman asserts his identity through his folk tradition. I cannot thank Lakshman enough for the many times we met until I could find my voice in his athma-kathe. I hope the original and the translation sound like a duet to someone who can read both Kannada and English.

I thank Mini for sharing my enthusiasm while translating *Samboli!*. Our discussions on the phone helped me dwell in the text in the spirit of a tapasvi. Fortunately for me, Mini does not know Kannada. Talking about the text to her enabled me to clarify my thoughts and hone my expressions even as I was in the throes of writing myself out. I thank Nirmal Kanti Bhattacharjee and Niyogi Books for readily accepting my translation.

My special thanks to my children and grandchildren and my many friends who shared my wonderment as I journeyed towards an enlightenment.

Susheela Punitha

Samboli: Travails of a Dalit Activist

V S Sreedhara

Lakshman's *Samboli!* is yet another addition to the growing body of Dalit autobiographies, which, in their content and form, have developed into a distinct genre of 'self-writing'. Being a poet and a story writer, Lakshman infuses his narratives with rich details and images which acquire metonymical dimensions. Steeped as it is in the dialect of his community, some passages are poetical in their use of the language. The translation has retained many native expressions, which are self-explanatory and provide a flavour of the original.

As a literary form, autobiographies have provided a testing ground for ideas such as authorship, selfhood and representation. For a long time, autobiographies were considered unique to modern western civilization, which provided an account of fully formed authentic modern western selves as compared to the self-writings of non-western cultures, which were usually discounted as immature and pale, underdeveloped shadows of their western counterparts. The notion gained legitimacy in the wake of the belief that autobiography, by convention, should reveal an interior self different from the public self. But what about those accounts of the self where the distinction between the 'private' and 'public' could not be maintained, where the personal itself became the public? Dalit autobiographies are marked by this non-duality between the two domains, since they brought to the public domain a personal self which had hitherto remained unknown or unacknowledged. In other words, Dalit self-writings invariably and necessarily turn out to be narratives of the community and not just of a 'private' individual. In fact, the self becoming a signifier for the entire community is the hallmark of every minority in India. In a way, it is what distinguishes the minority as a distinct social category. One need not go very far to see the point. An entire community is named and shamed for the inefficiency or weakness of an individual from the marginalized communities, whereas the same logic does not apply to a person from a 'mainstream community'. Have we ever heard of an entire upper caste, *as a community*, blamed because of some corrupt members of the community?

Likewise, the kind of distinction that a critic like Lionel Trilling makes between autobiography and fiction in the context of western literary tradition does not hold good in the case of Dalit writing. Trilling maintains that while autobiography is valued in terms of sincerity, a fictional work is measured in terms of authenticity. This distinction may not get reflected in a similar fashion in the case of Dalit writing. Who can vouch for the authenticity of Dalit experience, which is largely unknown and alien to the modern (upper caste/class) reader? It is quite possible that for an 'outsider', Dalit autobiographies may appear to have fictional qualities. On the other hand, to consider them as mere sociological data or anthropological material about Dalit life would be a gross misreading. They carry with them a cosmology emerging from their lived experiences, quite different from that of the mainstream received world views, which also contributes to their authenticity. For instance, Lakshman writes about how his community elders viewed Deepavali, a great festival of celebration for caste Hindus, as an occasion for mourning. They even have a story to explain why it should be so. Similarly, to say that the experience of growing up for a Dalit child is always filled with shame and misery is to miss out on inner modes of being that sustains them, despite the practices of discrimination they face. The renowned critic, late D R Nagaraj, has drawn attention to the 'power of laughter' working as a subversive element in Siddalingaiah's autobiography. One can trace these features in *Samboli!* too, particularly when Lakshman describes his childhood days filled with fun and misery, discrimination and camaraderie in equal measure. This part of the narrative offers subtle but strong insights into the various forms of shaming and ostracizing that invariably constitute both the physical and psychological experiences of a Dalit growing up in the margins of Indian society.

None other than Dr Ambedkar has delineated the material basis for such discriminatory practices. In his treatise on *State and Minorities*, he argues how minority is not a question of number, but a matter of social status. In his simple but forceful definition, minorities are those who have no access to land, labour and capital. Thus, the stories of those who are deprived of these three material provisions invariably become the stories of the community as well. Among all minorities, Dalits, or ati-shudras as termed by Phule, are the ones who are most deprived of these material conditions. The denial of material resources, according to Ambedkar, is the prime reason for their exclusion. It also explains why justice has been denied, almost as a norm, in every case of Dalit atrocity from Kilvenmani* to Khairlangi.**

Samboli! needs to be read in this context. It is at once a story of an untouchable Dalit boy coming of age, and a reflection on the social conditions of the community which is struggling to find its dignity and social justice. Interestingly, unlike other Dalit autobiographies set in remote villages with socially well-defined and self-contained spaces, the events narrated in *Samboli!* are set in the outskirts of the city, making incursions to the city now and then. In its setting, *Samboli!* is in many ways similar to Dalit poet Siddalingaiah's *Ooru-keri* (renamed as *A Word With You, World* in English translation), and the narration gives a glimpse into the growing metropolis from the margins of the city. It is generally believed that a city's impersonal life offers a kind of anonymity to the Dalits, and hence a breathing space. The inhumanness of the city, by a quirk of irony, transforms itself into a humane face for Dalits!

---

* Kilvenmani is a village in Nagapattinam District of Tamil Nadu. On 25 December 1968, forty-four Dalits (including five aged men, sixteen women and twenty-three children) taking shelter to escape the wrath of landlords were surrounded and burnt alive. They were labourers protesting for higher wages and improved living conditions. The carnage led to huge protest and nationwide condemnation. However, all the accused, who were from the landlord community, were acquitted by the court for 'lack of evidence'. Since then, Kilvenmani has remained a symbol of gross injustice and atrocities on Dalits in post-independent India.

** On 29 September 2006, four members of the Bhotmange family of a Dalit caste from Khairlanji, a village in Maharashtra, were murdered. Two women from the family, Surekha and Priyanka, were paraded naked and sexually abused before they were hacked to death. Fact-finding reports by human rights groups as well as by the government have recorded the involvement of police officers, doctors and local politicians to cover up the crime. Though six of the accused were given the death sentence by a lower court, the Nagpur bench of the High Court later reversed it to life imprisonment, arguing that the murders were carried out as an act of revenge and not for reasons of caste prejudice. For detailed analysis, refer to Anand Teltumbde, *The Persistence of Caste: The Khairlanji Murders and India's Hidden Apartheid* (London: Zed Books, 2010).

But not always so. Lakshman's story tells us how the 'human face' of the city is just a thin veneer, which frays easily once the real identity is known. The incident where Lakshman has to lose his government job captures this vividly:

> *It is only after I joined the Dalit Sangarsha Samiti in its struggle for justice and wandered through villages meeting other Dalits whose lives were on the streets like mine due to the malice of caste distinctions that I realized why I had landed a government job in the first place; what it implied when I sat among the other guests at the lunch arranged by the bridegroom's family and ultimately, why I had lost my job through no fault of mine.*
>
> *I understood why people of the upper castes do not permit Dalits to enter their homes, wells, hotels and temples; the problem was larger than what had happened to me as a person. I read the writings of Ambedkar, Periyar Ramaswami and the revolutionary, Basavanna. I got involved in the protests of the Samiti and experienced both victory and defeat.*

It is a telling comment on how modernity sits uncomfortably on the shoulders of our cities. Even today, it remains a sad fact that it is nearly impossible for a Dalit (or a Muslim, for that matter) to find rented accommodation in a big city like Bangalore. It also explains how the city's demography is mapped on caste lines, although all this seems to happen rather unintentionally. The term *samboli* refers to the public announcement of a Dalit's arrival in a public space so that others avoid his shadow. The practice may be visibly absent now, but its essence remains. It is like the cat's grimace in *Alice in Wonderland.* The grin remains even after the cat has disappeared!

Ambedkar had envisaged how caste prejudices would cut across modern institutions as long as they continued to be controlled by the upper castes. He had vehemently argued for the nationalization of all land and public resources, so that a secular state would ensure a fair and just distribution in housing and other related facilities. When we see how private layouts that have mushroomed in cities perpetuate caste prejudice and caste demarcation, albeit in a veiled way, we can realize how important it is for the state to take over land and housing.

Dalit autobiographies invariably vindicate Ambedkar's visionary analysis of the caste system, and *Samboli!* is no exception. It captures in minute detail how caste operates both in its sheer nakedness as well as in various hidden and insidious forms in the daily life of Dalits. Ambedkar has written extensively on how caste-based discrimination is unique to Indian society, both in its structure and operation. His famous statement about the caste system as not just a division of labour, but of labourers too is still a glaring reality. Caste operates through a highly intricate system of hierarchy, where various social groups caught at different levels within the hierarchy act both as victims and perpetrators of the system at the same time. Thus, each social group, even among Dalits, discriminates against the other subgroups by feeling superior to or different from other groups. Added to this is the ethical justification it employs to sustain itself. Nowhere else in the world, Ambedkar points out, do we see social discrimination provided with a moral value as it is done in the case of caste system in India. It is no wonder that the dominant castes look upon themselves as privileged by a divine will, as it were, to maintain the caste hierarchy. Thus, violence on Dalits, which is a daily occurrence even today, is seen as a just act, sanctified by the moral authority derived from tradition.

In Lakshman's narrative, there is an instance when he, as a young boy, is caught by a caste Hindu for stealing sweet tamarind (a wild fruit) and is inhumanly punished.

> *Towards the evening I had fever. I could not sleep that night. No one ever plants and grows a sweet tamarind tree anywhere at any time. It is a wild tree; it grows anywhere it pleases. While others gather its fruit to enjoy its sweet taste, we eat it to satiate our hunger. Then, why did this Narayanappa abuse me so badly? Why did he beat me up? Why did he make me clean the shit on his slipper with my shirt? Such questions pounded me like torrential rain. I opened my eyes. I felt as if I was seeing that Narayanappa dancing, thaka thai. I got frightened. I shut both my eyes with both my hands and slept.*

This episode recalls a similar instance in Devanura Mahadeva's *Kusumabale*, where a Dalit is tied to a tree and beaten up for stealing tender coconuts. On seeing this, a Dalit activist asks the owner of the garden, a caste Hindu, to register a complaint with the police instead of taking the law into his own hands, but is laughed at. In real life, there are stories which are more gory and sinister than this. It was not long ago that parents belonging to a dominant community in Karnataka killed their own daughter in cold blood for having married a Dalit boy. Honour killings are now a new norm, thanks to the ethical value attached to caste discrimination.

Lakshman, like most other Dalit writers in Kannada, is an activist and has been a part of the Dalit movement. But unlike many other Dalit activists, he is critical of its trajectory, particularly in the way it got mired in identity politics and groupism. The question of identity and representation is certainly valid, but it can either veer towards a fundamentalist position or take a progressive form. As Nancy Fraser points out, identity or claims for recognition of difference should not hinder the pursuit of social justice. To bring the two issues on a common platform is a big challenge of our times. Lakshman's story ends with this hope and awareness that they are two ends of the same spectrum. In fact, his autobiography documents the growth in his social consciousness when he joins the Karnataka Liberation Front and starts working for the eradication of caste with the realization that it can liberate not just Dalits, but all oppressed people. This is very pertinent, since the class basis for sociocultural oppression is an issue that cannot be pushed under the carpet anymore. One wishes he had written more about the activist phase of his life, for it would have thrown much light on the present crisis facing the Dalit movement. I hope he will bring out a sequel and record his journey as an activist.

We are living in troubled times where social activists are looked at with suspicion and even declared anti-national. Dalit writers and activists have many more challenges to face than they did during their childhood days. Even institutes of higher learning are no exceptions in perpetrating caste discrimination, as Rohit Vemula's (and many more Dalit scholars') institutional murders indicate.

The term 'samboli' means 'Warning! Dalit Coming!', and it seems to have now acquired new connotations. Lakshman's book sounds the warning in more than one sense of the term. The indications are already there in the form of recent Dalit Yatras carried out in Una village in Gujarat and Udupi in Karnataka for Dalit rights. The writing on the wall is clear, but are we ready to read it?

Kinship Terms

akka, akkayya, akko	: elder sister
ajji	: grandmother; also a way of addressing elder women
amma, ammayya, ammo	: mother
anna, annayya, anno	: elder brother; also a term of respect
appa, appayya, appo	: father, (ayya–suffix denoting respect; o–suffix denoting familiary)
athe	: father's sister; mother's brother's wife
chikajji	: grandfather's younger brother's wife
chikthatha	: grandfather's younger brother
maga	: son; also a term of endearment
makkale	: children
mari	: little one, a term of endearment
mavayya	: mother's brother; father's sister's husband
thatha, thathayya	: grandfather; also a way of addressing elderly men

SAMBOLI!

A life story by Lakshman

Translated by Susheela Punitha

'Unless a grain of wheat dies,

it cannot bear fruit.'

A Palace without Walls

Amma had taken me to Gaanigarahalli near Banavara for the village festival to honour the gramadevathe, the Goddess of the village. It is the village of the Ganigas, the oil-presser caste, and Amma's hometown; her parents lived there. During the festivities, I too ran across the smouldering embers in the devara konda, just as my ancestors had done before me; just as the other devotees were doing that day. After the festival, no one took me back home.

I was like the baby elephant in a story. *Once upon a time, there was a baby elephant. It was let loose in a roomful of sugarcane. That baby forgot its mother, its relatives, friends and forest; everything. It was that overjoyed with the sugarcane. When it had finished munching all of it, the baby elephant remembered its mother, relatives, friends, forest*...I too forgot my Appa, my Amma, relatives, friends, village...I lived happily with my Thatha and Ajji and their nurturing.

One day, as Thatha sat at the door weaving a rat-trap, an elderly man came up to him.

'What, Thatha? How're you? Who's this boy?'

My Thatha stood up flustered, dhadabhada, crossing his hands across his chest.

'How's it you've come this far, Swami? And that too in this burning sun. Come, come; stand in the shade here.'

Thatha welcomed him with great humility. Pointing to me, he said, 'He's my daughter's son, Swami. They'd come for the village festival. He's been here since then. His father has too many children. Too much poverty in that house. Here we're just the pair of us, mudhuka and mudhuki. And so I'm thinking of bringing him up here, Swami…'

'Arre, Thatha, do you have any sense? You're keeping such a fine boy at home and ruining his life? Is this fair? Anyway, you've spent your lives as ignorant people. Should these children too grow up like you, tell me now? Remember to bring him to school tomorrow and get him admitted. Understand…?' That sounded like a threat.

'Yes, Swami, yes,' Thatha said, bringing his palms together in deep respect.

Early the very next morning, Thatha washed my face, hands and feet, smeared my hair with castor oil and combed it down, smeared a tiny black spot of saadhu between my eyebrows as a caste-mark, handed me a slate and slate-pencil and admitted me in the school on the old mantapa, the village platform.

Next to my Thatha's hut was the hut of his younger brother, my Chikthatha. The pair of elder grandparents and younger grandparents were not on talking terms. My Chikthatha and Chikajji gave me plenty of things to eat whenever my Thatha and Ajji were out.

'Le, Lachma, why do you turn away even when we call you? What have we done to you that we shouldn't have done? Did your Ajji and Thatha ask you not to come to our house? If they've said anything like that, tell us, Maga…'

I don't know why, but my Thatha and Ajji scolded me if ever I went to anyone's house.

Thatha used to sell eggs. Every day, he brought me savoury snacks like karaseve and bonda and biscuits shaped like animals and birds; elephants, camels, crows, parrots…I played with the biscuits even as I munched on them.

I got all excited on Saturdays about going to the fair at Banavara. I walked ahead of my Thatha and Ajji, swinging my arms. Nature's songs of silence came humming through the casurina grove. It was music to my ears. I looked around, entranced, wondering from where the melody floated in; I could not make out. Birds twittered in the hedges, keech-keech. They fluttered away when I threw a stone. I stared at them until they flew out of sight.

'How wonderful it would be to soar like them!' The desire floated through my mind quite often.

I loved to see the lake at Chikbanavara fill to the brim and spill over during the monsoon. As it came in wave after wave to crash against the bank and melt away, I brought my palms together in obeisance to the water and said, 'Amma, Gangammathayi, our mother!' Even as I watched them, white cranes suddenly dived for fish into the water and disappeared into the distance. Snakes sunned themselves on the rocks on the banks of the lake. The breeze from across the lake filled me with joy. There was enough greenery all around to delight the eye and the spirit; shrubs and trees, sugarcane and paddy fields.

People from neighbouring villages came in waves to the Banavara santhe. This village fair was a feast for the eyes and an entertainment of sorts with tribal families coming to earn a little in different ways. Some brought trained monkeys all dressed up to dance and then to go among the spectators with a plate, begging for alms. Some were snake charmers who played a type of flute called the pungi to get the cobra to raise its bespectacled hood and look about this way and that, swaying to the music. They asked for an offering of milk and eggs to the cobra in return for amulets. There were those who played with gangetthu. They took a decorated bull, cow and calf around as Rama, Sita and Lakshmana. They asked Rama, the bull, 'Rama, will you marry Sita?' The bull would nod in response to a stealthy tug from his master, and one of them went around collecting money for the wedding. There were Muslims who did the kankattu. These were acts of mesmerisation based on faith, not reason. Calling upon the power of Allah, a man split a huge slab of granite into two neat pieces with one hammer-stroke of his bare hand; three men writhed out together through a small hoop. They begged for alms in the name of Allah, the Powerful. Some sold medicinal herbs and seeds to keep demons and illnesses at bay, and some others, poultry, sheep and goats. The bustle and excitement was beyond words.

After the fair, we went straight to the Banavara toddy shop in the evening, bought two bottles of toddy and something to munch with it like chaakna, slices of mutton grilled on embers without any spices, and such savoury snacks as bonda or seasoned boiled beans served on leaves. We sat in the open maidan, calm and relaxed. We brought our palms together, bowing reverently to the toddy, and shared it with Mother Earth together with some of the eats before we let our hands and mouths fight with each other! Ajji gave me a sip of toddy from her bottle and then Thatha gave me a sip from his. The toddy was sour and tasty. We munched the chaakna and the other snacks with it. Crows and squirrels came close to us, scrounging for leftovers in the scraps of paper littered about. I tossed them a little of whatever I was eating.

Thatha and Ajji never stopped with one bottle. They drank with ease until they were drunk and doddering. They teetered this way and that down the street with bags in hand and bags on head, mumbling, grumbling, scolding, barely in control. I felt strangely happy when I was drunk. My legs tossed about any which way, and I felt as if I was floating in the air as I walked. If I looked this way or that, Thatha or Ajji warned me, 'Be careful, Lachma! Look ahead and walk.'

Thatha's house had no brick walls. Toddy-palms fronds were held upright one beside the other, and a strip of bamboo held across the middle and bound with rope to hold the palms together. That was a low wall with four knee-length, branched trunks of trees as supporting pillars. A long trunk resting on taller branched trunks served as the main beam along the length of the house. Bamboo poles were tied to it on either side as crossbars on which rested a sloping roof made from the husk of crushed sugarcane, bound firmly with rope made from the fibre of an aloe-like plant. The house was never too hot, never too cold. In one corner was the fireplace. Beside it were the grinding stones; the small flat stone and the huge mortar-and-pestle kind. Next to it were pots piled one on top of the other size-wise with the topmost for drinking water. Towards the right in a corner were pictures of the gods. That was where the lamp-stand stood. That was where we ate. The door was a set of palm fronds set side by side, held in place with a strip of crushed cane and bound together with rope. The door had no lock. Whenever we went out, we held the door in place, tied it to the wall with a piece of wire and sealed the wire with cow-dung. To the right of the door were long stretches of rope-lines on which our sleeping mats were slung during the day. To the left was a lean-to that served as the bathroom with a granite slab as flooring and a loft to store firewood. Next to the bathroom was a fireplace to heat water. This small but well-kept hut was our palace.

Our house was filled with an aroma every Saturday evening; the God's lamp burnt from evening until we went to bed. Ajji brought her palms together prayerfully before she put out the flame reverently with the edge of her sari. Then the palace filled with darkness. And in the darkness of the night, the whole village hummed with the chirping of crickets…jyeeen. My bed was a mat of woven palm leaves piled high with rags stitched on to it and covered with a sheet. It was as long as I was. My pillow was a bundle of clothes. Thatha's hand on one side and Ajji's on the other patted me to sleep, while they told me stories of kings and queens, and gods and demons until I dozed off. I remember one of those stories even now. It was Thatha's story:

> *On a Marnomi (Mahanavami) night, I was walking on the bund of the Banavara lake near the grove where souls of the dead live. I was taking the gatey, a bottle of toddy to offer my dead ancestors. A dark darkness enclosed us. And I heard the dead spirits talking among themselves.*
>
> *"Enrappa…what? Had you been to your homes? How're your children, their babies, relatives, friends?" one asked another.*
>
> *"Ayyo, what can I tell you about the story in my house, appa?" the spirit replied. 'My daughter-in-law's very arrogant. She hadn't salted the meat curry she offered me today. I ate it all the same."*
>
> *"In my house, they had kept everything that's offered as ede to the dead," said another, "new clothes, items for the puja, food that I loved, toddy for gatey and betel leaves, nuts and tobacco. But they hadn't kept any sunna to chew with the betel leaves and areca nuts."*

'The spirits of the dead kept talking that way, Maga, each one narrating how their families had treated their dead. I felt so scared that I crept back home quickly. The gates of heaven are opened on every Marnomi day, the ninth day of the Dasara festival. We keep the ede on the feast of the Marnomi, don't we? The dead of our families come to eat it, Maga. And so, we must remember what our elders loved to eat when they were alive and serve all those dishes. When I die, you'll keep the ede for me, won't you?'

Every year on the feast of Marnomi, I remember the story my thatha told me. At the same time, I remember the words of the revolutionary poet Basavanna too: *There is no other heaven or hell; right conduct is heaven and misconduct is hell.*

During the night and during the day, I heard the train cross Chikkabanavara…jugubugu, jugubugu, cooo…The more I heard it, the more I longed to hear it. The joy brought me deep sleep at nights. During the day, I opened my ears wide and listened to the train chugging across.

Thatha and Ajji took me to my home town Kathriguppe for my elder brother's wedding. No one took me back to Thatha's house in Ganigarahalli. I lost a year of school. The next year, when I went to the school in my village, I was readmitted to the first standard. The palace where my ajji and thatha lived became a mere sweet dream.

'Maga, you have to come home for the Marnomi festivities this year without fail,' said my mother quite recently.

'Why, Amma?'

'You've settled down in Bengaluru. You haven't been offering the ede to your dead ajji and thatha. They've made your head that was that big into a head that is this big. They sent you to school and made you a person who can read and write. Shouldn't you return that runa, Maga? Don't you have an obligation towards them for making you what you are?'

'Amma, listen. How did you come here now from Kathriguppe? You came by bus, didn't you? My Thatha and Ajji have died in Ganigarahalli, haven't they? We've dug their graves in the graveyard and buried them in that same village, haven't we? And you keep the ede for their souls in Kathriguppe year after year during the Marnomi festival. Which bus will Thatha and Ajji take in the darkness of the night from the graveyard in Ganigarahalli to Kathraguppe to come and eat your ede? Paapa, poor things! Who'll give them the bus fare? Is it possible for the dead to come alive again, you tell me? What joy will the dead get from the way we build monuments over their graves and put out the ede for them to eat?'

My mother's face fell.

'Does that mean you won't put out the ede for us when we die, Maga?'

'No!' I said firmly. Tears flowed from my mother's eyes. She covered her face and wept.

'God, please give my son a good mind,' she pleaded fervently as she wept.

'Amma, look! It's my duty to bring you everything you want and take care of you well as long as you live. If I don't look after my Appa and Amma while they're alive and offer them the ede after they're dead, what's the use? It becomes an act of ignorance to do such things.'

Amma was not comforted, no matter how much I tried to comfort her. She continues to grieve.

Though truth is cruel, though it is unacceptable, I firmly believe that truth does not die.

Beggar Turned Poultry Farmer

Long, long ago, a white man had come to the Doddagutte hill near our village to hunt game. He died while hunting. The others who were hunting with him dug a pit right there, buried him and set a cross over his grave.

Countless Christians flock to the hill every year a week or two after Yugaadhi to pray at the cross on the grave. The way to that hill is a little beyond our slum. Soon after Yugaadhi, the children, the elders and the disabled from our colony await the return of the Christians, counting the days like the jaataka birds that swing upside down meditating on God. Because…on that day, the hands of our people jingle with coins—jana, jana.

'Swami, please give me three paise…three paise, Swami,' I begged on that day from early morning, standing in the pathway to the grave or trailing the visitors, pulling a sad face with my palm stretched out. As soon as someone gave me some coins, I dropped them into the pocket of my shorts and went to another group and begged, 'Swami, please, three paise…please…'

'We've already given,' some said. Some of them did not know our language. They smiled saying something. I did not understand them. Anyway, they never frowned at us; they never scolded us. And so, we never felt bad about begging from utter strangers.

Once, my classmate Muniraju of the Vokkaliga agricultural community and his father were walking along that way. I did not notice who they were.

'Swami, give me three paise, please...three paise,' I begged, going after them. The boy turned. Muniraju! I ran away embarrassed because they were from our town and from an upper Dalit caste. Since then, I made it a point to look closely at the person I followed before saying, 'Swami, three paise, please...'

On the day the Christians came to visit the grave on the hill, the path was lined all along the way with vendors selling watermelon and mash melon, ice candy and spicy snacks, eye-liners, whistles, flutes and other toys...Exhausted with begging in the burning sun, I bought ice candy, ate it hastily biting it bit by bit, wiped my mouth and, arranging my face in a sad expression again, I went back to beg, 'Please, swami, give me three paise...three paise, please...' On that day, my belly was stuffed with watermelon, mash melon, ice candy and whatever the Christians gave us; goodies we had never seen, never eaten. The next time I would get to eat so much would only be the following year when the Christians visited the grave again. They left for Bengaluru before the day was done. They would not give us any money on their way back, but that did not keep us from trailing them and begging. They just walked away briskly.

Exhausted with shining since the morning, the sun slipped softly behind the Dodgutte hillock. The cool evening breeze refreshed my body that was weary from a day in the sun. I walked towards Karegutte in the dusk. The flute I had bought for two rupees was tucked into my waistband. I was happy. My feet dragged. I lay flat on a rock, closed my eyes and played on the flute until I was tired. The Goddess of sleep was trying to sit in my eyes. Birds in the nearby shrubs accompanied my flute with varied notes. Darkness enveloped us. I touched the flute to both my eyes in reverence, tucked it again at my waist and walked homewards.

The gr…gr of the grinding stone sounded like the buzz of bees. Amma's voice was sweet, as she sang songs of the ragi that she was grinding into flour. The lilt of her song made me feel as if she was swinging me in the cradle again. I was happy. The oil lamp burnt peacefully on the dividing wall of the room. I kept it on the floor and pulled out all the coins I had stuffed into the pockets of my shorts and shirt. The jingle of the coins was music to my ears. It distracted Amma from her song.

'Appaappah! Where's all that money from?' She was astonished.

'That's what those Christians gave me.'

I stacked them neatly according to denominations: coins of five and ten paise and four annas. I counted the number of coins in each pile and wrote down the number in each denomination on a sheet of paper and added up the lot. The sum that day was sixty rupees and four annas.

Marakka came home to borrow a cup of ragi flour. Amma sifted the flour, filled it to the brim of a cup and handed it to her. Marakka whispered something in Amma's ear and began to wail.

'Don't cry, Marakka,' Amma comforted her. 'It's not good to cry once the lamp is lit in the house.' Then she came and sat beside me.

'Marakka's family is facing a lot of difficulties, Maga. They'll be selling their poultry tomorrow morning. They're willing to sell us two hens. Will you buy them for us?' she pleaded. I nodded.

Amma counted the money twice, and I counted it twice, and then we gave Marakka twenty rupees.

'God bless you, Maga,' said Marakka, laying her hand on my head. She tied the money safely into the edge of her sari, took the cup of flour and left. I counted the remaining money again, tied it in a handkerchief, put it safely on a shelf, ate a ball of ragi for dinner and went to sleep.

The darkness disappeared and daylight was laughing when Marakka came with a hen under each arm—one black and the other brown.

'Here're your hens, Mari,' she said, handing them over to me. Amma took the fowls and checked them, turning them this way and that. She let them loose in the yard, tying one end of a length of string to the leg of a bird and the other end to a piece of stone. Then she fed them a ragi ball, pinching bits of it, dipping it in water and throwing it to the fowls. I watched, giggling with happiness, as they pecked at their food and gobbled it up. I tried to touch them fondly, but Amma jumped at me as if she had stepped on a snake.

'Don't do that, Maga. Don't let the hens get used to human touch. There're some poultry thieves lurking around. They've spirited away Bailamma's precious cockerel and didn't let anyone get the aroma of that chicken curry. Paapa, Bailamma, she's weary with searching all over the neighbourhood, looking into every bush, scratching at every pile of garbage. She couldn't find even the feathers of that rooster. But how long will a stolen blessing last, after all? Thu, instead of living such a life, it would be far better to drown in some tank or well. Bailamma's family had preserved that rooster to offer it to Marammathayi, Maga. Wait and see! One day or the other, that Goddess will surely give them a clue to the thief. You too will see it with your eyes. As it is, the Goddess is like fire. The culprit will die spitting blood…' A lame dog came limping to get some of the pieces of ragi ball thrown to the hens. Amma chased it away with stones.

The fowls got used to us in barely three days. During the day, they would go foraging for food all over the neighbourhood and come home to roost for the night. I would be back from school and, without fail, get hold of them and put them under a basket for the night. I fed them bits of food before leaving for school. During vacation, I went to work on the piece of Thappatteyappa's farmland that my family farmed. There, I plucked ears of paddy from the Patela's fields and stuffed them in the pockets of my shorts for my fowls.

One day, the black hen was standing in the yard and making a noise as if it was clearing its throat. That meant it was ready to lay eggs. Akka came to the house clapping her hands and dragged me outside into the yard, saying excitedly, 'Ei, look here! Listen to that! Your hen is clearing its throat.' At that moment, Amma came from the well, balancing a mud pot of water on her head and another on her waist.

'What more, Maga!' she said, looking at me and smiling, as the hen kept making that grating sound. 'You've become a poultry farmer.'

Around that time, my maava visited from Thotadhaguddadhahalli, a village beyond the farm-hill. He chased after the brown hen and cut it up for a chicken curry. Now I had only the black one. It became doubly precious to me. I looked after it with eagle eyes.

One day, I found an egg in the barn and then one every day for twenty days after that. Meanwhile, the hen sat in a corner making a strange noise—kor, kor…Amma got Malakkajji, an old woman, to set the eggs in a basket for the hen to hatch them.

She set a coconut shell of moistened ragi near the basket in the dark corner for the hen to eat. She picked some kedhage flowers and left them in the basket to keep away the lice that come with hens. Amma listened keenly for sounds from that chicken coup. She marked the passing days on the wall with a piece of charcoal, a line for each day. Early one morning, there came the sweetest sound from the coup—piyapiyapiya…Amma quickly brought the lamp towards it. By the time the sun rose, we could see all the twenty chicks. She put them all in a winnowing tray. When I tried to touch the chicks in my excitement, the mother hen rushed to peck at me.

'Give me one of the chicks, Lachma. I'll look after it as mine,' Akka begged.

'Hoon,' I nodded.

Even as a raw fruit ripens, even as a calf becomes a bull, the chicks became fowls right before our eyes. The Marnomi festivity was at the entrance of our village. Except for the mother hen, Appa took all the twenty fowls to the market in Bengaluru and, with the money earned selling them, he got new clothes stitched for all of us for the festival.

We placed the metal utensils in the house in the hall and worshipped them. We placed the ede for the ancestors. We wore new clothes. We ate meat dishes to our fill and enjoyed ourselves.

'Thanks to you, we had a great Marnomi festival this year, Maga!' Amma praised me with all her heart.

The people in the neighbourhood called me Koli Yajamana, the owner of poultry!

Illness

An illness plagued me until I was about fourteen or fifteen years old. During every monsoon, especially whenever I got drenched, I would break out in hives from morning until around ten at night. The swellings on my body were tiny, the size of lentils like avare or alsandhe. The people of our village call them pothevu.

Whenever the swellings came on during the night, I sat in front of the open fire and warmed my hands, my legs; my whole body. I heated the metal blower in the fire and gently rubbed the soles of both my feet with it. Slowly, the hives would disappear. Then I slipped into a gunny sack and slept snugly. Whenever the swellings erupted in the mornings, I went to Durgamma's temple, leaned against the wall near the door, stretched out my hands and legs and sunned myself facing the sun. The swellings came down as soon as the heat of the sun warmed my body. If I saw the sun trying to hide behind a cloud, I called out:

Cloud, O Cloud!
Disappear.
Sun, O Sun!

Come here soon.
Sunshine, O Sunshine,
I'll give you butter
Come to me brightly.
Sunlight, O Sunlight,
I'll give you ghee
Warm me up gently.

Some elderly person had told my mother that the medicine for hives was pathre. She stole the pulpy leaves from some houses near the market and brought them for me. I ate them. They were spicy hot. She also gave me some native medicines together with the herbal leaves.

An eccentric pujari who did not seem to be a priest in any temple came to live in our settlement. He leant against the wall of the Durgamma temple in the mornings to sun himself. He removed his jubba and spread it out in the sun. As lice crawled out from the creases of the warmed shirt and ran helter-skelter in panic, he caught them one by one and crushed them between his thumbnails. Then he loosened the drawstring of his shorts and killed the lice hiding there.

If anyone brought the puja items to the temple, he got up immediately, got some water from one of the houses, washed his face, hands and feet and sat down to conduct the worship. He danced wildly whenever Durgamma entered him. He thrashed himself with a cane. He rid others of demons.

'Who are you? Why have you come? What do you want?' he asked, screaming.

Those who were ill and those who had lost jewellery came seeking flowers from God. It is a belief that the petitions of the devotees found favour if the flower fell from the right side of the idol. It was a bad sign for the flower to fall from the left. The devotees decided for themselves whether they would be successful or not in their venture.

Whenever anyone in our slum lost cattle, calf, fowl, metal pot, plate, axe or sickle or anything else, the crazy pujari would point to the direction in which it was taken when the Goddess was upon him.

'Tell me, O Devi, will I get back my jewellery?' the devotee asked.

'No, you won't. It has gone far away, crossing the village. It is the handiwork of a woman or a man or a child,' he replied.

Trusting the words of the demented pujari, the petitioners suspected everyone and cursed everyone—even their husbands and children. They cursed anyone with 'you dwarf, my son; you, beanpole of a son; you childless widow; you gutless fellow who can't take care of your wife; you husband-deserting shrew; you offspring-eating demon. You white cockroach! (Their contention was, how can a dark Madiga's child be fair unless it is illegitimate?) Everything about anyone they suspected was cursed and scolded indirectly; their character, height, weight, illnesses, health, wealth, pet names, ancestry…The suspected person knew for sure that he or she was being targeted and a quarrel ensued, ending up, at times, with fistfights, involving the whole settlement.

One day, when I was sunning myself by the door of the Durgamma temple, that crazy pujari came and sat beside me.

'Le, mari,' he said, addressing me as a child, 'if you want to be rid of these hives, make a vow that you'll toss the sweet-smelling dhavna herb and bananas at the deity in the chariot during the Karaga procession at the Dharmaraya temple in Chickpet in Bengaluru.'

The people in our settlement implicitly believed that the gods filled the pujari's whole being and spoke to us through him. We held him in great respect. And so, his words filled my heart with joy to the brim. I ran home immediately, washed my face, feet and hands, stood before the picture of the deity with my feet and palms together in obeisance.

'Swami, paramathma!' I vowed fervently to the Supreme Soul, 'Take the hives that swell up all over my body. I'll throw up a bunch of dhavna leaves and bananas to you as you ride your chariot on the day of the Karaga festival.' My respect for the pujari grew in leaps and bounds, for he had shown me a way out of my suffering.

One day, the Goddess had entered the pujari and he was dancing in wild abandon. She heard the joys and problems of the people and advised them through him. Maranna was drunk by the afternoon. Swaying and stumbling and dancing like the pujari, he kept asking stupid questions. The Goddess in the pujari got angry and hit Maranna's head with a coconut. Wherever the anger was, it came upon Maranna like a demon. His eyes were like burning torches of fire. Gnashing his teeth, he stood holding a stone, impervious to the people trying to calm him down.

'Stop! Take your Durgamma out!' he roared as he chased the pujari beyond the precincts of the village.

A rumour spread all over that that would be the end of Maranna; that he would die spitting blood. It reached the settlements where Maranna's relatives and friends lived. Maranna and his relatives were filled with terror, whether awake or asleep.

'Have you seen our crazy pujari?' they asked anyone who visited our village. 'If you set your eyes on him, you must tell us without fail, please,' they pleaded, bringing their palms together.

There was a legend woven around the pujari: *As a boy, he was a cowherd. He took cows and calves to graze in a jungle nearby. Once, an orthodox Brahmin was worshipping Kali near a huge medicinal shrub known as the ekka tree. Chanting a mantra, he cut his finger and offered the blood to the Goddess. No human being was supposed to see the ritual, but this cowherd had watched it. The vaidika called the boy to him, cut a slit in his thigh, placed an amulet in it and sutured the slit…*Thanks to the power of the amulet, gods possessed the crazy pujari from time to time. He could do good or he could do harm, depending on the whims of the spirit possessing him…he filled the villagers with fear.

I had written the final sixth-grade exam. We were having our summer vacation. Bettanna of our village took some of the boys from the slums to work, where some streets were being tarred in the new extensions in Bengaluru city. I pleaded with Bettanna and managed to go with them as a daily-wage labourer. But he paid me less than what he paid my younger brother.

'What is this, Anna? Is Nanja older or I?'

'He's an old hand, Lachma. Can you work the way he does? Whatever it be, you're educated, more refined…' That shut me up.

One day, I filled tar in a can with holes and swung it back and forth to spread the tar decoratively on a road in Jayanagar. One of my classmates happened to walk by. He came up to me and said, 'Ei, how're you? When are the results expected?' I felt as if the boiling tar had splashed all over me. I bent my head, ran to the mixer mixing tar and scree and hid behind it.

'God! Who else will see me working here as a coolie? When I go back to school, these boys will look at me and laugh among themselves, won't they? God…!' In my heart, I wept.

I got my wages on Saturday. I put the money in my pocket and secured it with a pin. The house was ridden with bugs. All of us were sleeping outside. As the cock crew before dawn the next morning, people from our slum came, waking us up to go to the Karaga festivity in Bengaluru city. They called out to this one and that one. I too walked with them. By the time we reached Hanumanthanagara, the sun was rising. My hair had grown up to my neck. A barber was opening his salon right then. I stared at the shop longingly. He was doing the puja, circling scented joss sticks in front of the few steps to his door.

'I need a haircut,' I thought to myself, staring at him. 'But I wonder if he'll cut my hair if I ask. What if he scolds me? What should I do?' I stood there wondering. The barber finished the puja and looked this way and that before setting eyes on me. He saw me from head to toe and grumbled something to himself. I saw his lips muttering. Then he waved to me. I went up to him. He looked this way and that again.

'Do you need a haircut?' he asked.

'Hm,' I nodded.

He wrinkled his face and gave me a haircut, holding his nose from time to time.

As I walked along, I saw a house under construction and, beside it, a tank brimming with fresh water.

'What if I wash my head here?' The idea surfaced. 'But I don't have any soap…' I walked on briskly until I saw a shop where I bought a piece of washing soap. I walked back to the tank, stood beside it and looked this way and that. I could not see a single soul. I coughed a few times and even cleared my throat loudly. I did not hear a single voice. I guessed no one was around. Growing bold, I sat on my haunches, cupped my hands and poured water on my head. I soaped myself and rubbed it all clean. I patted my head with both hands, patapata…I powdered a bit of brick, brushed my teeth with it and washed my face.

Then I strode away proudly. I touched my hair from time to time. It was as smooth as peacock feathers. My heart was happy, but my body shivered in the cold. My teeth chattered.

Countless chariots of gods and goddesses were adorned in front of the Jayachamarajendra Market. Two eyes were not enough to see the hustle and bustle of the people who had come to be a part of the Karaga festivity. I took aim and tossed the dhavna herb and bananas at the kalasa placed on the chariot. My offerings did not touch the sacred metal pot. Again, I got the sweet-smelling dhavna and bananas, thought about god and threw them, but again they did not touch the kalasa. For the third time, I got the dhavna and the bananas, touched them to my eyes with devotion, thought of all the gods and goddesses and aimed at the kalasa. They touched it. My heart filled with an inexpressible sense of peace and joy.

'Swami, paramathama, I've fulfilled my vow to you. Please see that I don't get those hives again,' I prayed fervently. I went to another chariot and offered worship. I smeared my forehead with the red and yellow bhandara powder given to the devotees. I stuck a flower behind my ear. I received the mangalaarathi and touched it reverently to my eyes. I bowed humbly in worship and smacked my cheeks in penance. And then I bought a whole lot of savoury and sweet snacks like kadalepuri, kaaraseve, pakoda and kajaya and stuffed them into a bag. I also bought bananas, khol and a rattle.

Someone was serving buttermilk and limejuice sweetened with jaggery and boiled pulses in front of a shop. I stuffed myself. My doddappa and doddamma came and drank the buttermilk and limejuice and ate the boiled gram. They came again and again to collect the gram and store it away in a bag. People squabbled over the bits of coconut that fell and scattered as they were broken in front of the idols on the chariots. My uncle and aunt too were among them. They went wherever rice and curry or buttermilk and limejuice was being distributed, collected the rice, curry and boiled pulses in bundles and, placing them on their head, went about looking for other charitable units serving food.

I slunk away from them. I felt it was a disgrace to gather more than what we needed to assuage our hunger at that moment.

It was midday. I bought a pair of dark glasses that was nothing more than circles of red cellophane paper stuck to cardboard rims and tied with a rubber band that went round the head to hold the 'glasses' firmly in place. Then I walked back home with my bag in my left hand and my rattle whirring away in my right hand.

My mother's face became like the full moon as soon as she saw me.

'Amma, Amma, remember I had vowed to toss dhavna leaves and bananas at the kalasa on top of the chariot during the Dharmaraya's Karaga festival if I was cured of the hives? I did it! I aimed at the sacred pot and threw them! My offerings touched it!' I said.

'Swami, paramathma! Bless my son, Appa,' prayed my mother, bringing her palms together in front of the picture of the deity.

Pork was being cooked in the cattle shed, filling the house with its delicious aroma. My father handed me my share of liver that had been roasted and set aside by the fireplace.

Relatives who lived in the neighbourhood came home every year for the Dharmaraya's Karaga festivities. And the relatives of our neighbours too visited them. The people of our colony slaughtered sheep, pig and fowls. Somehow, they also managed to get toddy. Our neighbourhood looked like a village fair. That day, I ate ragi ball with mutton curry. I was happy to have fulfilled my vow to the deity. I was relieved; I would never be bothered by hives ever again. I sat on the platform in front of the house. I became drowsy. I fell over, curled up and slept. When I woke up, the sun was a red ball of fire in the east. The whole expanse of sky was red with laughter. The clouds too were laughing, shaped like animals like the elephant, camel, horse and bear and some birds. The wealth of that sight brought joy to my heart.

The Lord of the Rains

Maleyraaya, the lord of the rains, had gone into the forest. Rivers and lakes were parched and cracked. Water from the well was slushy. It was many days since we had seen the face of a proper meal of ragi balls and greens curry. Once in the morning and once at night, we cooked some half a seer of horse gram with some salt, shared it amongst ourselves and drank water. Our jaws hurt with chewing gram. For months on end, my tongue did not know the taste of anything else but that salted pulse and water.

Now and then, a buffalo or a cow died in the village. They brought it to our settlement, chopped it up and distributed it among the families. Then a sense of well-being danced on the faces of our people. Every kitchen fire was lit. With our share of meat, we made curry with as much as we needed and sun-dried the rest in a basket and stored it away for other days to be munched as a side dish with ragi balls and curry. And we would wait, wondering when the next cow or buffalo would die. The people in our colony became breathing corpses. Joy and laughter became a dream.

Then early one evening, Byranna came running from the village, breathless.

'Come, everybody, come!' he cried, 'The Gowda of the village has sent for us, come! Come and gather at the Durgammathaayi temple.' He went around the settlement, shouting out the announcement. All of us gathered near the temple of our Mother Goddess Durgamma.

'Listen, everyone,' said Byranna softly, 'The people of the upper castes in the village worshipped Maleyraaya for seven days, pleading with Him to send us rain, but not a drop has fallen to the earth, and now they are starving, chewing on stray grains of rice. So they want *us* to appease Maleyraaya. All the important people in the village are asking us.' Exhaustion stole the rest of his words from him. Bylappathatha's high-pitched voice took over from Byranna.

'Yes, what will be the plight of men and dumb animals if it doesn't rain, if we don't have a harvest?' he wept. 'Let the boys get together early tomorrow morning and worship Maleyraaya our way. If He condescends to descend and fill the earth with His fullness, we can survive at least as labourers somewhere or the other.'

That evening, all the boys from our settlement raced one another to gather at the Durgammathaayi temple grounds and blinked at each others' faces wondering what to do next.

'Go and get everything ready,' Bylappathatha's commanding voice rang out. The very next moment, Nanja appeared through an opening beside Ninganna's house. He hoisted a shard of tile on his shoulder, as if it were a mace, and stood like Anjaneya, the Monkey God. I went into the sanctuary of Durgammathaayi's temple, put some turmeric and vermilion powders on a piece of paper and looked for incense sticks. I found a few used ones and a fresh one. I got them all and stood beside Bylappathatha. Byranna's son, Chikka Byra, hung a drum from his shoulder, held a long stick in his right hand and a short one in his left and came running to stand beside me.

'Look, makkale,' said Bylappathatha, 'you must go and return as one mother's children. Go to our village today, go to Kallasandra tomorrow; go to some other village the day after. Do what you have to do and return.' His hands swayed like the hooded heads of cobras. All of us went towards Donkalahalla, the pit where the idol of the Rain God would be created.

Muniyappa, the pujari of our settlement, took a lump of clay, put it on a slab of stone and kneaded it well with his feet, folded his palms in reverence to the lump and then made an idol of the Rain God with it. He took out two marbles from the pocket of his pyjamas and stuck them into the idol's face for eyes. The elders decorated it with flowers and smeared it with the arshna and kumkum powders I had taken. They did the mangalaarathi with incense sticks, waving them before the idol. All of us bowed before it one by one, bringing our palms together reverently. It was pitch-dark everywhere around us. Some stray glow-worms twinkled here and there. It looked as if Maleyraaya would get up and set forth in the glow of the oil-soaked torches. Looking at Him that way, I was filled with fear and devotion. Like everyone else, my heart too was beating fast, eager to carry the Rain God in procession.

'Le, Lachma, you can carry the Maleyraaya today,' the pujari said, looking at me. Tears came to my eyes. I stood with my head down. 'Say something, you dumb bull!' he shouted. My throat was dry, as I could not accept the honour.

'This is the only pair of shorts I have, Anno!' I cried. How could I get it wet?

Dhadum! Bettanna jumped into the water immediately to take my place. He sank and surfaced thrice, bowed in reverence to Maleyraaya, rolled the strip of cloth on his shoulder into a ring, placed it on his head and stood ramrod straight.

'Govinda! Go-o-o-vinda!' everyone chanted. We hoisted Maleyraaya on Bettanna's shoulders. The drumbeats reached right up to the neighbouring villages. The torches lit the way through the settlement. Every house in the slum welcomed Maleyraaya with an air of great festivity, washing the idol with water, smearing it with turmeric and kumkum and worshipping it with incense sticks and sending it on with gifts of rice or flour or money.

My heart overflowed with devotion as I taught the boys to sing to Maleyraaya:

Rain, O rain, O Maleyraaya
The flowering plants have no rain.
Come, O come, O Maleyraaya,
The banana plants have no rain.
Come pounding down, O Maleyraaya,
The guava trees have no rain.
O, come to us, O Maleraaya!
O, pour on us, O Shivaraya!

The boys repeated the lines after me joyfully, and we wended our way to the village. My Vokkaliga classmates made their way through the crowd towards me to touch me and to pat my back. They stood in front of me and grinned. They talked to me for no reason at all except to talk to me. My throat was parched with singing songs to Maleyraaya; I wanted some water, but did not have the nerve to ask for any. Generally, the Vokkaligas look down on us; the mere sight of us irritates them. But today, every man, woman and child of that community looked on us with deep respect and affection. We visited every house in the village without omitting a single one. Bellichukki, the star beside the sun, was twinkling in the west. We left Maleyraaya in the Donkalahalla pit, brought our palms together bowing reverently and returned home.

The next day we carried Maleyraaya to Kallasandra. By the time we visited every house in Kallasandra, sank the idol in a tank and returned to our settlement, the early rooster was crowing, kokkarakaa, ko! We measured the rice and the flour and counted the money offered to Maleyraaya. We handed it over to the elders and went back to our homes.

On the third day, as usual, we made an idol of Maleyraaya at the Donkalahalla pit and were heading towards Haavalahalli, beating the drum and singing the rain songs. We were barely half way there when the skies opened; thunder and lightning descended to the earth and drenched it with a heavy thunder shower, bringing a calming chill to every plant and shrub, bird and animal and every person.

Even as we watched, we saw streams of water flowing in from the ten corners of the world, meandering excitedly… seductively sludgy. We left Maleyraaya at Donkalahalla, bowing to him reverently. We were thoroughly drenched and, however hard we tried to make headway through the slush, we could only inch our way homeward like tortoises.

The palm fronds that served as the thatch-roof of our huts had flown away in the wind and were now resting contentedly in the fields and on the tops of houses. The roof was leaking; there were pools of water on the floor. Mother had placed pots and pans where rainwater was dripping. The drips made a musical sound, thot, thot. All of us huddled together in one corner. Mother had given me my share of ragi roti with a dry chilly to go with it. My whole body trembled in the chill—gadagada. I chewed the roti bit by bit and washed it down with water. The shivering got worse with the cold water.

'Stop, Maleyraaya swami, stop,' I prayed, 'Enough of your roaring rain! Spare the humble homes of poor folks like us.'

The rain stopped after a long time. My mother emptied all the pots and pans of rainwater and wiped the floor clean with a rag and spread a mat made from the fronds of the toddy palm. All of us lay down. A deep sleep swallowed us.

The wall of the house had slumped a little towards the end where the cattle were tethered.

'God is great!' said the people in our neighbourhood, gathering at the break of dawn, 'Thank God, nothing untoward has happened. What if the wall had crumbled on the children?'

We could see the sun, the moon and the stars right from inside our house.

The Power of Karwada Thanni

Once in a way, there would be quarrels in our settlement. People fought over children, fowls, dogs, whatever, and stopped whenever some elder or the other scolded them. Petty misunderstandings exploded into huge brawls, particularly on the day after Yugaadhi and on Mahanavami. These were days of festivity and celebration when meat was eaten and toddy drunk. Even as the green betel leaves, brown areca nut and stale whitish quicklime mingled in the mouth to make the fiery red mixture, petty excuses never failed to rake up old hurts that flared up into huge fistfights on these holidays. The quarrels usually began between one house and another and soon spread like filth among all the families, raising a stench in the settlement.

The elders in the neighbourhood gathered those who started the fight and advised them.

'Even if your spittle hits the ground accidentally in front of those who have a grouse against you, they'll think you're spitting there deliberately to insult them, Appa. And so you must learn to live cautiously. Nothing is permanent. None of us can carry away anything with us when we die. People must say, "Here lived a blessed man!" when we go. We must live without getting stuck in another's mouth, in another's hands…' The elders told the quarreling families to conduct themselves with propriety and made them exchange the thambula of betel leaves and areca nuts as a token of truce.

Someone somehow showed the people of our settlement a shop in Narasimharaja Colony, where they sold an illicit brand of country liquor called karwada thanni. Our people bought the liquor secretly and smuggled it into the settlement after sunset in fear. They poured it into an old earthen pot, added water and a little tamarind and salt and kept stirring it for about ten to fifteen minutes, holding the base of the pot firmly. Some smooth sticky stuff, much like tar, settled at the bottom of the brew. In a day, it hardened like stone. If anyone had a wound, they came looking for the house where the karwada thanni was brewed. The brew healed wounds when poured over them. It was inflammable; dhug, it caught fire and burned when exposed to fire. When it was stirred really well, clear water, like rainwater, rose to the top. People strained it with a piece of cloth and gulped it down like a drink with something to eat on the side. If they did not have anything else to munch, they chewed on salt crystals and drank it sip by sip. Their joy was unbounded if they were able to get karwada thanni on days when fish or crab or meat was cooked in the house. Then they would dodder about. If it became too heady, some curled up to sleep wherever and however they were. Some others shuffled and staggered about for a while, stuttering and stammering, scolding someone or the other, spoiling for a fight. Then muttering something to themselves, they too would slump like the dead to sleep it off.

'You're burning the gut in your belly with it. You'll die... You'll drive your children to the streets,' wives grumbled as they washed their hands and force-fed their drunken husbands.

The fire that falls upon a house takes the next one too as oblation, so goes a saying. Even so, quarrels that erupted in one home or the other spread to the next and the next involving brothers, families, friends...Every day, everyone fought like dogs, scolding, screaming, beating, pawing, crying, wailing. The stray dogs in the settlement and the foxes in Karegutte and beyond howled until they too were spent, until their voices too became hoarse.

'*Who's* that widow's son that got you people used to drinking this disgusting karwada thanni?' grumbled the elders.

Those who had created a ruckus during the night, scolding and quarreling unfairly with some others, found them at their doors quarreling with them for picking up a fight for no reason. And then we would know that day was breaking.

'Oh, let it be, Amma. Let them be, Appa,' said the elders who gathered to pacify them, 'Let whatever happened in the night belong to the night. You too scolded and spat on him last night, didn't you? Even if you don't wish to see his face, you have to see his back at least, haven't you?'

Once it became bright, the same people went about on their own, seeing to their jobs like dumb bullocks.

Every evening, I faced the setting sun and, bringing my palms together, prayed, 'My swami, keep my family from going to fight with anyone else. Keep others from coming to our house to pick a quarrel with anyone in my home.'

It must have been around five to six months since the people of our settlement started to drink karwada thanni. Well-grown adults and young men began to look like karwad, the sun-dried fish. They also developed a whooping kind of cough. Not one house in the settlement had a healthy person. Some of them suffered for some time and died right before our eyes. Relatives fell upon the body and wailed.

'What happened to him?' asked the people who came for the burial.

'Some worthless evildoer got our people used to drinking that karwada thanni, Appa. He went down drinking it, Appa,' wailed the family, beating their heads.

Whenever there was a death in the settlement, all the wage-earners would sit around the corpse. The fireplace in the house of the dead would not see fire that day. The landlords from the village would come in the night and scold them for missing work.

'There's been a death in our colony. We'll come early in the morning.' Our people pacified them, sent them away and then sighed, 'Those who've gone are blessed; we who're alive are the cursed.'

One night, there was a fight about some misunderstanding between my elder brother and Maranna who lived opposite our house. Maranna had plenty of relatives. Most of them befriended him for the sake of the booze he got them. Maranna had a loud voice. In a drunken rage, all of them beat up my father, my mother and my elder brother. Though my brother was locked inside, he somehow managed to come out and hit Maranna with the hittukolu. He cracked his skull open. Maranna's people came again and beat up my people. They beat up my father until he almost died. My mother went weeping and beating her breast all the way to the village and complained to Thapatteyappa's children, Byranna and Ramanna. They knew us; we farmed their land on lease. They came right away, holding flashlights. Seeing that my father could hardly stand, Byranna said, gnashing his teeth, 'You, you sons of whores! How could you raise your hand against a godlike person?' He kicked up quite a ruckus, kicking and beating up all of Maranna's people. Munirajappa, who worked for Maranna for daily wages, also came and beat up Maranna and those who sided with him. All of them pacified my father.

Mysteriously, the bottles of karwada thanni disappeared. The brawls in our settlement dwindled and died down. But even now, when I see someone squabbling, scolding or drawing blood, my limbs tremble. I remember the days when my people drank illicit liquor and picked up needless fights.

Thefts at Dusk

When I returned home from school, I placed my books on the dividing wall in the house, tossed a towel over my shoulder and crept out to stand like a green snake at the door of the Durgammathaayi temple.

Narayani too came to the spot. Looking furtively this way and that, we went thieving together.

'Where to? Let me come too,' asked someone or the other walking by.

'Nowhere in particular; we just happen to be here.' I would halt and sit on my haunches. Narayani would pull down his pants and look for a place a little distance away.

Once we were walking along the Chikbaavi road. Should that Chikbyra too happen to come that way? He must have been spying on us and guessed what we were up to. I sat down right there, wondering what to do; we could neither take him with us nor leave him behind. What were we to do?

'Shall we play the mud-game?' I said, gathering the mud on the road into a little pile.

'Le, you robber, my son! Did you have to come this far to play that game? You guys are trying to shed me somehow and go robbing some farm or the other. And you're trying to smooth talk me into believing you, are you? I'll go with you wherever you go today, you schemers,' he said, as if challenging us to shed him. He even sat cross-legged in front of me!

I gathered the mud into a longish pile, broke off a piece from a twig and shuffled it about in the mud before leaving it hidden somewhere in the mud-pile. Then I cut the pile into three units and said, 'You fellows take whichever pile you want.' They pointed to the ones they had chosen as theirs. The stick was in the pile left for me; I won the game. I won the second game too. Narayani won the third game. Chikbyra won the fourth.

'Cheating! Cheating!' cried Narayani, 'This fellow knows in which pile he's hiding the stick. Let's start all over again.' He ruffled all the piles.

'Le, you rascals,' said Chikbyra, angrily, 'You're shamming the game, aren't you? One is covering up for the other! Can't I see that? But just remember this: a thief who robs for ten days will be caught one day or the other. I'll see it with these very eyes, you wait and see.' And he walked away, abusing us.

'Come, Narayani, let's go home. Somehow, the signs aren't auspicious today. This idiot was after us to check us out,' I said. We were walking along the mud-path leading to the big well. Ragi had grown knee-high in the fields on either side. As we walked, we plucked a few sheaves, pulled the grain from them, rubbed them between our palms to remove the husk from the grain, blew the husk away and tossed the millet into our mouths.

'Le, look around…See if anyone's coming,' said Narayani, suddenly going down on his haunches. He quickly took a few sheaves from either side of the pathway and tied them together at the ground level and ran away. Both of us sat atop a slippery rock some distance away and watched like hunters, eyeing their trap anxiously for a catch.

Soon, a trail of three women came along that path with pots on the head and at the waist. The first one tripped and fell on her face. She wailed aloud, hitting her head. The two of us laughed until we were sore. We did not move from our perch on the sliding boulder until the sun set and darkness covered our eyes.

We were familiar with every fruit tree that grew at its own pace in the fenced orchards. We also knew in which season the fruits of which tree would be ready to eat; guavas, jumblums, dates, mangoes….We knew where each tree was. We sneaked up towards the trees, looked this way and that, made sure no one was around and gorged ourselves with fruits that were on the ground. We prowled around the orchards all the time. When one of us slunk into the farm like the green snake, the other kept watch beyond the fence. If we spied anyone's shadow, we slithered into the undergrowth.

We stole whatever we could lay our hands on, vegetables and fruits. We bundled them firmly in our towels and dangled them at ground level as we walked. If we spotted anyone, we dropped the bundle right there and walked away from it down another path. Later, we took them to Kanneerkatte and hid them close to the fence or in mounds of earth. If we hid them under the fence, rats got at them. If we covered them with mud, the rains would flatten the mounds, making it difficult for us to spot them later.

Stealing was easy, but enjoying the things we stole was very difficult. Everyone who saw the bundle in the towel asked us, 'What's in it?' If ever the children of the Vokkaliga community saw our booty, they forced us to open the bundle and show them what we had and then grilled us: 'What is this? Who gave it to you? Where did you get it from…?' A hundred and one questions! If they got suspicious, they abused us; they beat us up and took away our spoils.

Sometimes, when it was not convenient to rob anything else, we went to the garden beyond the water tank. Standing on the tank bund, we could see the shrubs of the kedige in bloom. To reach the garden, we had to walk through a marshy pit. By the time we walked through the slushy, thorny bushes, we had forgotten where the kedige shrubs were. On locating them, we climbed the trees. As we climbed, we were scared because baby cobras were supposed to live in them. Anyway, we climbed the trees, picked the flowers, hid them beneath the fence and, marking the spot, we walked away looking innocent. But our faces, hands and feet gave us away, for they were decorated with scratches like the fine lines of rangoli designs that decorate our homes.

We woke up early in the morning, washed our faces, hands and legs, smeared some ash from the fireplace on our foreheads and taking our spoils of fruits, vegetables and flowers in a bag and our books in our hands, we went via Kanneerkatte towards the vegetable vendors who sat by the roadside in Narasimharaja Colony to sell our supplies and buy a breakfast of dosas or idlis with meat curry before going to school. We shared whatever money was left equally between us. We tucked the money near the drawstring of our shorts, so that no one would notice it. If we needed any money, we went to an isolated spot and pulled it out deftly from the waist.

We used to carry out such thefts at least once a month. Once, Narayani and I were walking stealthily near a rocky hillock next to Thappatteyappa's farm. The land darkened bit by bit as the sun closed its eyes. Our eyesight dimmed. Our hearts trembled. We took each step hesitantly. I broke out in sweat, imagining cobras and pythons. I prayed silently to Anjaneya. We waited until we saw my parents and Thappatteyappa's family going home after the day's work on their farm. Then Narayani and I jumped the fence and stole whatever we could lay our hands on; tomatoes, cucumbers, string beans, papayas…Then the dog Ramu spotted us somehow, perhaps by smell. Bo, bo, bo, he barked as he came towards us. His bark was loud enough to be heard in the next village. I went towards him quickly. 'Hey, Ramu, come here. Quiet!' I said, petting him. The dog wagged his tail.

We were creeping warily into the farm, step by step, when Thappateyappa's sons Byranna and Ramanna, and Byranna's son Venkateshappa spotted the two of us.

'Some sons of whores have taken to raiding our farm,' they were talking among themselves, 'They look like boys. If I get my hands on them, I'll kick them and leave them floating in the well.'

They were particularly furious when papayas were stolen. When they cursed our parents as well with foul expressions, I felt like crying. My heart thudded. I broke out into a sweat. Every word they spoke fell like a lash of the cane on my heart.

'Thu, I should never go thieving this way again. I should never hear such curses again,' I vowed to myself. But my decision wavered whenever our fireplace went cold, whenever my belly beat the drums of hunger.

Once, when there was yet a tinge of twilight, Narayani and I crept into Thammayappa's farm and ransacked a patch of vegetable marrow. Bundling the marrows in a towel and tossing the bundle over our shoulders, we wormed our way through

Narayanappa's sugarcane field and edged along the bund to a marshy pit that was safe enough to jump down and make good our escape.

Suddenly, Munirajappa appeared in front of us like Yamadharmaraya.

'What's bundled in those towels?' he asked.

Frightened, Narayani tried to flee, but lost his balance on the bund and fell into the water canal beside it. Munirajappa caught hold of the two of us. I was trembling. My tongue was dry. Munirajappa spilt the vegetables in the towels and bound my right arm to Narayani's left arm and walked us towards the powerhouse in their field, kicking and beating us and dashing our heads against each other. There, he tied us to a cart with a rope. He beat us with a cane until welts began to appear. We bawled out, beating our mouths. The dog that was tethered to the bars of the window of the powerhouse too whined aloud with us, 'kuyoooooon!'

Venkateshappa, the grandson of Thapatteyappa, happened to come there. Munirajappa complained to him about us robbing his vegetable marrow, clobbering us all over again for good measure. I could feel the welts when I touched my cheeks.

'This one's our Muthu's son,' said Venkateshappa, recognizing me. 'He's studying in Bengaluru. He's not the type to steal this way. He's been with some outsider and learnt to do such things. Let go of him this once.'

'Bloody thieves, they are! They must've seen a fox's face today to be so lucky. Or else, they would be standing here the whole night. They would've shit in their pants by daybreak,' said Munirajappa, knocking our heads together again for good measure. 'If you step this way again, I'll chop off your legs and hand them to you,' he warned.

After we had come a distance, I caught hold of Venkateshappa's feet, pleading and crying, 'Please don't tell my appa or my anna about this, Anna. I'll never do such a thing ever again. Honestly, I won't.'

I writhed like a fish out of water. I was in such anguish.

'Don't have anything to do with boys like these. Take care!' he warned me and hit Narayani on the head. That night I ate my meal of ragi ball and went to bed, but I was worried. What if Munirajappa told people that I had stolen marrows from his vegetable patch? What if they called me a thief? Anxiety and fear were wrung from me like water from a freshly washed piece of clothing. Sleep stood far from my eyes. My father snored like a storm, but I tossed about from side to side.

Dogs were barking somewhere in the distance. Would there be thieves lurking around? I wondered. As the first light of the morning touched the earth, I remembered an incident that had happened in our settlement a long time ago:

Munivenkatappa's goat had entered Munirajappa's vineyard. Munirajappa's farmhand Mara caught and slaughtered it and was found out. Our people shaved his head, smeared three stripes of quicklime on it and laid the entrails on it. They hung the goatskin, the goat's head and legs on him and paraded him through the neighbourhood. He was so disgraced that he left the village. The image of Mara's humiliation came to me in waves like heavy gusts of wind. I was scared that I too was in a similar situation. I broke into sweat, though I had not covered myself. Thankfully, at some point, without warning, sleep swallowed me.

Early the next morning, I walked towards Karegutte. The sun was rising in front of me over the hillock. The earth was awash with sunlight. And yet, the disgrace of stealing the vegetable marrow and getting caught covered me like the darkness of a new moon night.

That was the last time. Narayani and I stopped robbing the farms and orchards. Whenever the two of us got together on our own, we would say to each other, 'So, how was it? How did it feel when the hot, hot kajjaya fell?' referring to the walloping we had got and laughing at our plight.

'Le, don't ever go falling at someone's feet, Lachma,' he would say to me.

'And don't *you* go falling into the canal again,' I would tease him in retaliation.

For many years after, Narayani and I laughed over this one incident.

The Festival of Defilement

During Deepavali, the boys of our colony went out as a group to sit in the open fields from evening to midnight and gaze towards the village in the gathering darkness and bone-chilling breeze, forgetting food and water.

And then we heard the burst of crackers from the village, dum, dum, damaar. When a spray of sparkling colours burst upon the night sky, we shouted, 'O!' and danced about clapping our hands. Crackers like the airplane and rocket drew beautiful designs on the dark sky. Then we would shout, 'That's mine! This is mine!' If one of us tried to own a flare of design that someone else had already appropriated, we would quarrel over the ownership.

'Look at the way you're fighting over someone else jewellery. What if it had been yours…? Stop it, you idiots!' An elder advised us, seeing us squabbling.

'Come on, boys…come home to survive on ragi ball,' some other elder shouted at us. And we shuffled back to our homes unwillingly. On Deepavali nights, I would see the burst of colour in the night sky even in my dreams.

As soon as we woke up the next morning, the boys from the colony made tracks to the streets in the village where the Vokkaligas lived. We went looking for half-burnt crackers among the colourful debris of the previous night. If we found any, we stowed them away in the pockets of our shorts. If I ever happened to find a cracker with a wick, I felt as happy as if I had found a fortune.

'Look here! Look here! I've found a brand new firecracker!' I shouted, prancing about and showing it off to everyone. I treasured the new ones in my shirt pocket. Together with the firecrackers, we found some scented sticks as well. After making sure we had got all the bangers we could, both used and fresh, we returned to our colony bustling with excitement. While we were scrounging around for them, the Vokkaligas tried to drive us away, scolding and threatening us. Their children made fun of us.

We gathered around the Durgammathayi temple and tried to burst the crackers we had gathered. We pulled out the hidden wicks and lit them; some fizzled out, tuss, some burst, damaar. We cackled as loudly as the bangers boomed. We frolicked, we somersaulted; we enjoyed ourselves. We emptied the gunpowder into a neat little pile and lit it; it went burr. The flowerpots dazzled us with a colourful flourish. We went homeward after burning them all, the ash black on our fingers. We rubbed our hands with sand to wash it off.

When I was in seventh grade, I gave up looking for firecrackers during Deepavali or standing in front of Vokkaliga houses with a cane basket during festivals.

On one Deepavali day, Venkateshappa, the grandson of Thappatteyappa, took me to his Athe's house in Chikkakallasandra. Some boys got talking to him even as we entered the village; all of them spoke in Telugu.

Right there was an idol of boor-boor Maramma sitting in a basket. The image was bedecked with flowers and smeared with kumkum and turmeric powders. A whip lay on the ground. The man carrying the idol was dressed in a skirt of many colours. His chest was naked. His body was full of welts. He went from house to house begging, while chanting some mantras and whipping himself. Hence the scars. He was feeding something to a girl. There was a woman in front of him with a kind of drum called the thamte hanging from her neck and a stick in each hand. As she rubbed the sticks against the sides of the drum, they made that noise, boor-boor.

Some mean fellow crept up behind me and pulled down my knickers. It slipped to my feet. I pulled it up quickly and tucked it back into my waist-string. My mother had got the shorts for me from some house in Narasimharaja Colony. It was multicoloured. The material was tough. It reached down below my knees. But it was also baggy. Another boy too could have fitted into it. Holding on to it with one hand, I traced my steps behind Venkateshappa's, looking behind to see if any of those scoundrels were stalking me.

'Stay here by the door,' said Venkateshappa, as we reached his athe's house. 'Keep looking out to see if anyone's coming to taunt you. If they do, call out to me, Anno. Don't stand there like a dumbo. Hushar! Take care!' With that, he went inside.

I was edgy. 'What will I do if those fellows who disgraced me at the entrance to the village come here?' Such thoughts and fears bothered me. I looked around. Venkateshappa used to give me a few coins from time to time. A question arose in me, 'Won't he give me some today? That too, when he has brought me from one village to another?' A feeling of confidence answered it, 'He'll give me some; I'm sure.'

After a long while, Venkateshappa and his athe's daughter emerged from inside. They were giggling like lovebirds and stepping outside together like twin bullocks. She was still laughing as she handed me a ten-rupee note, saying, 'Buy some firecrackers.'

On our return, Venkateshappa gave me different types of crackers and sparklers and flowerpots that were still in sealed packets.

Early the next morning, I was bursting crackers in front of the Durgammathaayi temple. All the children of our colony milled around me.

'Ei, give me one…give me one,' they begged.

'Burst another cracker…just another one,' they pestered.

I moved them to a safe distance and lit the loudest bomb, the Lakshmi pataki. Our colony shuddered.

'Who's that idiot?' shouted Pillakkajji. 'Don't you know you're frightening the cows and calves? Go to the fields.'

Bylamma's son Chikkabyra was bothering her to get him some firecrackers too.

'Le, mari, please give my son a cracker,' said Bylamma, stretching out her hand.

'I can't, Akko. If I give one, I'll have to give all of them.' I was engrossed in lighting a firecrackers.

'O, there's no end to his arrogance! He acts as if he's bought the whole stack! He must've picked them up from some bylanes of the village,' Bylamma made a face at me.

'Ammo, why do you talk like that? Look at them! The packets are sealed.' I proudly pulled out my stock of brand new fireworks from my pockets and spread them out in front of Bylamma like a slap on her face.

Bylappathatha was sitting in front of his hut. He had matured in wind and rain, heat and cold.

'Le, Mari, come here,' he called me. I went to him.

'Sit down,' he signalled. He stroked my head lovingly as he would stroke his pet puppy. 'I thought you were a clever boy, Lachma,' he said, 'but you're holding this inauspicious thing in your hands and burning it right here, inside our slum. It's not proper for you to be doing that. Don't do it.'

I felt as if someone had poured steaming hot water on me.

'What wrong have I done? Why is this old man saying this to me?' I wondered. I worried.

'Why, Thatha? What did I do?'

The old man cleared his throat, spat and said, 'Once, on the feast of Deepavali, one of our ancestors had gone to a village fair to get the puja done for the noma. You know the red string tied round the wrist during Deepavali? That one. And also to buy the ingredients for the sweet kajjaaya made for the festival. He never returned. Here, everyone's eyes became holes staring down the lane…watching and waiting for him. They didn't know what to do without their elder. They felt helpless. They were plunged in grief. That's why we consider the festival of Deepavali as a sutka, Mari; it's a ritual defilement. The firecrackers are ritually impure for us. They are untouchables. We shouldn't burst them, can't you see?' He completed his story and asked, 'Can we celebrate the festival that took the life of our ancestor as a sacrifice? You tell me now.' He looked me in the eye as he asked me this question. His face was drawn; his eyes looked worried. I took all the firecrackers I had and tossed them into the garbage pit. I have never touched a cracker since then.

Bylappathatha's question has dwelt with me and worked on me in different ways as I have sought answers to it.

Most of the workers at the firecracker factories are children. Whenever I hear about them losing a hand or a leg or their very lives in accidents, I grieve for them. I feel as if I have seen the mutilated bodies of these poor people in the flamboyant colours of the crackers. I see the destruction of the environment in the clouds of fumes. I see those with money burning crackers and enjoying themselves, while those without fortune pining because they cannot afford them. I have learnt about the differences among people and decided to work against them.

For a start, however, I wanted to be a model; I gave up bursting crackers.

I have since learnt that the purpose of burning crackers on Deepavali, the festival of lights, is to burn away the darkness within us; the darkness of evil desires, pride and arrogance, deceit, corruption…selfishness. If this be true, then our bestial nature should have become ashes with the annual burning of crackers, shouldn't it?

But obviously, such good principles do not affect the communal mindset of our country. The proof is in the injustice meted out to Dalits in the form of exploitation, oppression, murder, extortion and every other kind of abuse. The sun and the moon neither rise nor set without seeing such inequities every day.

Bylappathatha had a point in telling me that the festivities at Deepavali were a ritual defilement to us; that the bursting of crackers was a ritual pollution.

It may be a way of protesting that we do not want what we cannot have because Dalits, anyway, have no way of celebrating any Deepavali ever with good food, new clothes and crackers; we just cannot afford them. Though we do back-breaking work, the fruits of our labour have only been half-filled bellies and raggedy clothes because we have no right to land or production.

A society built on differences has never ever considered us, Dalits, as human beings.

It could also be a way of fostering an upper-caste notion that Dalits should not observe any of their festivals.

Unless those who believe in humaneness come on to the streets to condemn such despicable practices, the lives of human beings will have no meaning. Unless people internalize the truth that idealism has to be practised, not worshipped, it is pointless to celebrate Deepavali as the festival of lights or to burst crackers to dispel darkness, year after year. If we want to dispel the darkness within us, we have to incinerate our desire for deception, hatred and vengeance the way we burst crackers. We have to enlighten our hearts with a people-centred truth that respects human dignity. Only then will human life have any value.

O, Deepavali of polluted light, when will you become a pure light for all people?

The Harvest

That year, the ragi crop was ready for harvesting. For two days, the hearth in our house had not seen fire. For two days, the sun was lost in the sky. The rain kept pouring in torrents. Cattle, calves and people hesitated to stick out their heads. With all that dripping, our house had pools of water collected everywhere. We had no place to sit or stand. For two days, we had not seen the face of a ragi ball; our bellies were rumbling. We had drunk water the previous night before going to bed. Sleep was scared to come to us because of our hunger. I was famished. The disgusting cold kept me trembling, however much I tried to curl into myself.

After a while, I began to feel queasy. I did not have the strength to even cry; I kept tossing about. Amma gave me some water to drink. It worsened the nausea. I was retching without throwing up. I felt I was dying. I felt dizzy. My eyes grew dim.

'Ayyo, devare!' my mother cried out to the Supreme Being, 'My little one is dying with nothing to eat. What shall we do now, paramathma?' She hit her head as she wept. Appa went out in the rain without asking anyone, without telling anyone. After a long time, he returned with sheaves of ragi in each hand.

'I'll fry the ears of the millet, remove the husk and give it to you, Lachma. You can eat it and go to sleep,' Amma comforted me. Quickly, she lit the fire, heated the ears in it, put them in a winnowing fan and rubbed them. She winnowed the ragi, blew away the husk and shared it into seven neat little mounds in plates, lids, whatever. Each one of us ate a pile of the millet and curled up to sleep, wherever we were, however we were. The cocks began to crow, cockkakko, ko! Though the sun was high up in the sky, my comforting sleep would not let go of me.

The following Saturday was a half-day at school. Byra, Nanja, Narayani and I from our colony sat on the hillock, Karekalgutte, and plotted to creep in stealthily and raid our landlord's ragi fields.

'Who are those sons of whores?' We heard a woman's voice threatening. The four of us bounded like deer, jumped the fence and ran away in four different directions. After a while, Byra whistled from the hillock. We gathered there again.

'Ei, what shall we do now? Our plans misfired!' Narayani's voice was hoarse.

'Let's raid Sunkenalli Gowda's field,' suggested Nanja. We separated and went alone to different parts of Sunkenalli Gowda's ragi field. Nanja climbed up a neem tree and looked around. Then, he signalled to us. We crept in under the fence, plucked out sheaves of millet, keeping an eye out for one another and edged out of the field, hiding the sheaves behind our backs. We jumped into a pit for safety and laughed at one another. Poor Byra had thorns in his feet. I pulled them out.

'Ei, listen,' said Nanja, 'Anyway, there's no one in the field. Let's break off some of the fencing to make a wood fire to roast the ears of ragi.' Nanja and I trod softly towards the fence and brought back a few pieces for firewood. By then, Narayani had managed to get a few matchsticks and some red chillies.

The fire was crackling. We were cackling as we warmed the ears of ragi in it.

'On what shall we rub the ears to separate the husk from the millet?' asked Narayani.

Everyone looked up and down. I quickly took off my shirt and spread it on the ground. Eagerly, we heated the ears in the fire and rubbed them on my shirt. I felt pinpricks on my bare back as the merciless sun beat down on it.

'You know what happened yesterday?' That was Nanja. All of us stared at his eyes and mouth. 'This Brya's father had got drunk stealthily by the afternoon and come home with a bottle tucked into the pocket of his shorts. He stood in front of his house.

'"Pray, tell me, my minister, do we have good rains and a good harvest in my kingdom?" he recited lines as if he were playacting. "Are my people happy?"

'"Besh, besh!" cheered the music master, waking up suddenly from his sleep on the platform outside our house.

'Byra's mother, incarnating immediately as badrakaali, emerged from the house like the demon, caught hold of her husband's hair, whirled his head about like a grinding stone and thrust him aside. He fell like a handful of dung, thapak. He looked as if he had fainted. I got frightened and went towards him.

'"Ei, what're you looking at, you rascal! Is there a monkey dancing here for you to be staring with eyes and mouth wide open?" She came towards me and I jumped from that place and disappeared in a flash. Or else, my head would've been tonsured like Thimmappa's, the god of Thirupathi.' He laughed, rubbing his head. We too laughed aloud with him.

Byra tried to hit Nanja with a sheaf of ragi. Sparks from the ember fell on Narayani's lap. 'Ayooo!' he shouted, dusting them off. A piece of ember shot out and landed on my shirt, burning a hole in it.

'This is my only shirt and now you've burnt it!' I hid my face in my hands and wailed aloud. 'How can I show my face at home now? How can I go to school?' My friends comforted me.

'Le, toss the sheaves into the fire,' Brya said. He too was tearful.

I was hungry. I was weepy. I wept until I was tired of crying; I could not console myself. We roasted all the ears of ragi, rubbed them to remove the husk, mixed bits of red chillies into the millet and divided it into four neat piles for the four of us. They added a little more to mine. We filled the pockets of our shorts and shirts and ate all we could. We lay on the Karigutte rock until the sun set and it began to grow dark. Then, we crept back to our homes.

The next morning, my mother patched up the hole in my shirt, scolding me all the while. I wore it that way to school.

'While trying to eat sheaves of ragi, he's burnt a hole in his shirt, this king of ours!' teased my classmates.

A Bitter Memory

That day, some four or five of us had gathered at the door of the Durgammathaayi temple.

'Who'll join us for a game of marbles with gejje-kayi?' asked Nanja.

'I'll come,' said Byra.

'Lachma, you be in my team. Let him get whoever he wants in his,' Nanja said to me. I did not stir from where I sat. Nanja handed the round seeds to me.

'Take,' he said.

'I won't play, I'm hungry.'

'Then, let's all go and find something to eat,' suggested Nanja.

'Listen to this!' Byra began, 'Yesterday, I'd been out with my father to get grass for the goats. How can I describe the wealth of the sweet tamarind tree? It was full of parrots, screeching—keech peech. As I was watching that tree, there were squirrels fighting among themselves—keey keey. The tree was laden with bunches of sweet tamarind. I got down the pit carefully and went towards the tree and what did I see?

The ground covered with sweet tamarind! I picked them up and ate them. I looked upwards at the tree and I just had to say to a parrot, "One for me, gilirama!" and the fruits fell as if the parrots had tossed them down to me. I ate to my heart's content,' Brya finished his yarn.

'Who'll come to raid the sweet tamarind?' asked Nanja. All of us looked longingly in the direction of that tree. Brya's little brother Chikkabyra tried to follow us with baby steps.

'Go and put on your shirt, Chikka,' Byra tried to send him home. 'We'll wait for you until you come. Come soon. If you go without clothes, a demon will get hold of you.' The little boy went homeward, looking back from time to time. As soon as he turned the corner near Ninganna's house, we ran away.

Our colony is below Karegutte. A cart track ran beside it. All the water from Karegutte flowed down into the ruts, deepening them like drains. The water that flowed down the ruts gathered into a pool. Beside the pool was a peepul tree. Stones with snakes carved on them were installed for worship under the tree. There was supposed to be a village there long ago. No one went near the tree because a two-headed cobra was supposed to live there. And right next to it was the grove of sweet tamarind trees.

We went hand in hand and entered the grove in the pit carefully. It was as deep as the height of some four or five men standing on each other's shoulders. We were picking up the tamarind on the ground when Narayani said, 'I'll climb the tree.'

'Don't talk, you blustering idiot,' Nanja spoke in a hoarse whisper, 'Someone might hear you.'

We collected all the tamarind we could, came out of the pit and sat in a circle under a toddy palm tree nearby. We put together all we had and divided them equally into four little stacks of tamarind and began eating, each from his stack, chatting about this, that and the other.

'I'll tell you a riddle. Let's see who'll solve it,' I threw out a challenge.

'Oho, I'll solve that,' said every one of them.

'Once upon a time, there was a town. Maleraaya, the king of rains, did not come to that town and so there was no harvest. A farmer was journeying towards the next town, deciding to make a living there. He had a goat, a tiger and a bundle of grass with him. On his way, he reached a pond. Now this farmer has to reach the goat, the tiger and the bundle of grass to the other side. How does he do it?' I challenged them.

'Let him take the tiger first to the other bank. Then, let him take the bundle…' suggested Byra.

'Then, won't the bundle of grass and the goat be on this bank when the farmer takes the tiger across? The goat will eat up the grass,' I cautioned him. 'You guys have to suggest a way in which nothing gets eaten.'

They turned the problem over and over; they scratched their heads, they closed their eyes, they rested their cheek in the palm of the hand. They looked this way and that….

'You tell us,' said Nanja finally.

'Yes, you tell us,' Narayani too begged.

'See. The farmer first takes the goat to the other side and tethers it there. Is that okay? The tiger and the bundle are on this bank. Right? Can the tiger eat the grass? No. Then he takes the bundle of grass across to the other side and on his way back, he brings the goat with him and tethers it on this side. Then, he takes the tiger to the other side and leaves it there. Is that okay? Now the goat is on this side of the pond. The tiger and the bundle are on that side. Can the tiger eat the grass? No.

Well, finally, the farmer takes the goat to the other side of the pond. Is that okay? That's all there is to it,' I said and sat quietly. The boys were stunned; they were happy. But, immediately, they realized the value of going to school; their faces fell and they were sad.

Somehow, Narayanappa of the Vokkaliga community happened to come upon us like a green snake. We ran helter-skelter. I ran towards the smooth sliding boulders, climbed them, jumped into the pit beyond, jumped fences and ran. Narayanappa chased me like a hunting dog chasing a deer and caught up with me. He too was exhausted; he was gasping. He tried to scold me, but could hardly speak. He waited to get his breath back…'Did you think you were enjoying the sweet tamarind from your mother's husband's land, you sons of widows?' He scolded me and thrashed me as if I were a mad dog. He kicked me into a pulp. He had lost his slippers while chasing me.

'Come and look for my slippers, you son of a Madiga!' he said. Abusing and kicking me, he brought me back to where we had been sitting, enjoying the tamarind.

'First, I came from this side. Then, I ran towards that side,' Narayanappa was talking to himself. I was sobbing away, wiping my tears from time to time.

'Ei, my slippers are lost. Find them for me, your mother's son!' He kicked me in the waist. Dhabaak! I fell on my face. I hurt my head. I could feel the bump. I cried louder.

'Don't try your tricks with me. If you don't find my slippers, I'll crush you with my foot on your neck!' he said, gnashing his teeth. Clenching my teeth, I looked for his slippers. The tears in my eyes blurred my vision of the ground. I wiped them away from time to time. He did not let go of my hand. One of the slippers was on the uguni shrub that spreads on the ground. I took it down for him. He slipped one foot into it. I could not find the other one. I was worn out looking for it.

Narayanappa looked as if he remembered something. He talked to himself. He dragged me towards the west. There was the other slipper lying in a pit. I felt as if I had got back the life I had lost.

'Anno, there it is!' I shouted. I got into the pit. The slipper had fallen on fresh shit. I picked it up. It was stinking. Narayanappa was furious. His face reeked vengeance. His eyes were bloodshot.

'Wipe it off, you son of your mother!' he hissed between clenched teeth, hitting me on the head. I did not know with what to wipe it. I stared at Narayanappa.

'Why are you looking at my face, you thief?' he roared. 'Take off your shirt and wipe the slipper clean with it!' Quickly, I took it out and wiped the slipper clean with it. Some of the poop stuck to my hand. I rubbed my hand on the shirt.

'Smell the slipper and see if it's stinking,' he said. I smelt it. There was just a little stink in it. I shook my head to say it was not smelly. I put the slipper on the ground. Narayanappa let go of me. Holding my shirt, I raced bareback from that place without looking back.

My friends who had come stealing the sweet tamarind with me were sitting on the Karegutte boulder. They whistled at me. I went there and told them everything. After listening to my story and looking at my plight, Byra kept whistling continuously. Narayanappa stood under the toddy palm staring at us. Seeing him, Byra took off his clothes and started dancing naked—thaka thai. After watching us for a while, Narayanappa took his towel off his shoulder and, tying it round his head, walked away towards the village. I spread my shirt on the boulder and wept. Narayani brought a pot of water. I washed it and spread it out to dry. I put on the clean shirt and walked back home.

Towards the evening, I had fever. I could not sleep that night. No one ever plants and grows a sweet tamarind tree anywhere at any time. It is a wild tree; it grows anywhere it pleases. While others gather its fruit to enjoy its sweet taste, we eat it to satiate our hunger. Then, why did this Narayanappa abuse me so badly? Why did he beat me up? Why did he make me clean the shit on his slipper with my shirt? Such questions pounded me like torrential rain. I opened my eyes. I felt as if I was watching that Narayanappa dancing thaka thai. Frightened, I shut both my eyes with my hands and slept.

Shravana Saturday

We are supposed to belong to the ancestry of Ventakaramanaswami. We have the ritual of doing the upaadhane by receiving alms from at least three houses on as many Saturdays as there are in Shravana, the fifth lunar month. This practice has come down for generations in our family. Chikkanna, the younger of my elder brothers, carried out the ritual in our home. He worked as a labourer in the house of the headman of the village. On Saturdays in Shravana, he got permission to finish his work and come home early to seek alms in Bayaagna. Whatever be the time, whatever be the weather, whether cold or rainy, he poured hot or cold water over himself and smeared the three vertical lines of white and red caste-marks on his forehead; the caste-mark that we put only during the month of Shravana. Then he smeared the same three lines on the chombu, the metal pot he took with him for begging. He reverently brought his palms together before the photographs of the family gods and the chombu and set out.

Every Saturday, Amma swept the floor and the front yard, and smeared fresh cow-dung diluted with water all over it. She washed everything she used in the kitchen: the mortar and pestle, the grinding stone, and the hittukolu-mettukolu wooden rods used for making ragi balls. She drew decorative rangoli designs on the fireplace and smeared it with dots of turmeric and kumkum. She drew rangoli on the front yard as well. She trimmed the wicks on the lantern and lit them. She wiped the dust off the pictures of the gods with a damp cloth. While returning from work at Bayaagna on Friday evenings, she would steal flowers from here and there and bring them home stealthily, make a tiny slit in a bit of a broomstick, thread a bit of thread through it, thread the flowers into strands and hang them on pictures of the gods. She wound a strand around the lamp stand as well. She lit the lamp and a few scented sticks. Our home was like a temple on Shravana Saturdays.

One Shravana Saturday, it was well past evening and close to the time for making ragi balls, and yet Chikkanna had not come home. Tired from walking back and forth like a bull at the oil press, Appa came inside and sat down leaning against a wall, grumbling to himself. If he heard a dog barking near the door, he shot out of the house and looked about, wondering, 'Why hasn't this son of mine come home yet?' Appa and Amma were as restless as ants in oil, talking to themselves. I stood by the light of the lamp on the dividing wall, memorizing a poem in English.

'Le, Lachma,' Appa said, 'Your chikkanna doesn't seem to be coming tonight. You better do the upaadhane. Go beg for alms in three houses.'

Amma was busy at the fireplace, feeding the fire with fresh pieces of firewood. She stood up immediately.

'Yes, Lachma, come, come. Nothing should come in the way of our duty to God,' she said as she held my hand, took me outside, stripped me and poured cold water over me from an earthen pot. She rubbed down my body, hands and legs with her hands even as she called out to my elder sister, 'Thayamma, get me the stone to scrub his back.'

Appa could not sit quietly. He came outside, grumbling about Amma, 'Big housewife she is, this widow! It's nearly time for demons to be wandering around, and she asks for the stone to scrub his back!' He was worried that it was getting a bit too late for me to go begging, but Amma was not intimidated.

'Is this any kind of life, a life without soap or soapnut? The child studies in town. Shouldn't he at least have some soap?' She kept muttering as she poured water over me again, brought me inside and, with the pallu of her sari, gave my wet head a good rub before wiping my face, hands, legs and the rest of my body. She got me into my shirt and shorts, stuck two scented sticks in my hands and made me wave them in front of the pictures of the gods Anjaneya, Lakshmana, Rama, Sita and Venkataramanaswami. By then, Appa had tied a strand of flowers to the neck of a chombu. He drew three lines of nama as caste-mark on my forehead and on the metal pot. I worshipped the chombu, held it in both hands with reverence and stood outside the door of our house.

'Shriman Narayana Govindaaa...G-o-o-ovinda!' I shouted. My whole body was trembling.

'Govinda,' responded Amma, as she came outside and put a handful of flour into the pot. 'Go now and beg in three other houses, Swami,' she said to me.

The darkness was dense. I stood in front of my doddappa's house.

'Shriman Narayana Govindaa...Go-o-o-vinda!' I stammered the chant as my trembling lips swallowed the words. No one came outside. I shouted again, louder, 'Shriman Narayana Govindaaa Govinda!' Doddappa came to the door.

'Don't they need their gods, these people? Has their work become so important to them? Look at them begging for alms so late in the evening,' he grumbled awhile and then he asked me, 'Don't your appa and amma have any sense?'

Dodamma put a handful of flour into the chombu. I turned the corner from the house and stood in front of my chikkappa's house.

'Shriman Narayana Govinda...Govinda!' Chikkamma came outside and dropped a coin into the chombu. I went to a side, took out the money and put it in my pocket, saying to myself, 'I can buy something to eat at school tomorrow.' The dogs kept barking. Appa kept following me at a distance, shouting at the dogs.

I completed the ritual of begging for alms without missing a single house, came home, placed the chombu in the room and brought my palms together before it in reverence. Amma set before me a steaming ball of ragi straight from the fireplace and beans curry, saying, 'Eat it and see that insects don't fall into your plate. Wrap yourself warm and sleep off.' I gobbled up the ragi ball, drank some water and curled up on the mat.

'Henceforth, you do the upaadhane every year, Lachma,' Appa said.

The following Friday, I took my books and was about to leave for school when Amma said, 'Remember, you'll have to go begging tomorrow. Come home this afternoon. Let's wash your clothes.'

And so, at lunch break, I went to my class teacher KSK Madam and said, 'Teacher, Teacher. Can I go home?'

'Why?'

'I have to do the Shravana Shanivara tomorrow, Teacher. And so my mother said, "Come home early, Lachma. We have to wash your clothes while the sun is still out."'

'Okay, go.'

I ran home from school, never stopping anywhere, never even looking back. Amma was waiting, looking down the street. She took my books from me as soon as I entered the house and placed them on the dividing wall. She unbuttoned my shirt and handed me a bed sheet.

'Wrap the sheet around you and give me your shorts,' she said. I wrapped it around my waist, pulled down my shorts, handed it to her and sat in the room.

'Come, Lachma, let's go and play marbles,' called out my friends.

'No, I won't.'

'Ei, Come on! What's this? Covering yourself with a sheet like an old man?' They caught hold of the sheet, trying to pull it off me.

'Ammo, Ammo! Come and see, come and see!' I shouted for help. Amma came inside.

'Look at him, Akka. We're asking him to come outside to play marbles with us and he's sitting here with a sheet on.' That was Janjeeva.

'Let him be, children. He won't come today. He has to study.'

Early on Saturday morning, Amma heated a pot of water for my bath. Tucking a piece of cloth to the cord round my waist, I sat outside and had a good bath, scrubbing myself clean with a piece of stone. Then, smearing the three lines of the caste-mark on my forehead and on the chombu, garlanding it and the pictures of the gods, waving burning scented sticks in front of all of them and sticking the sticks in the chombu,

I stepped outside our house and chanted, 'Sriman Narayana Govindaaaa...Govinda!'

Amma stepped outside with a handful of flour and put it into the chombu, chanting back, 'Govinda!'

Right then, Doddappa was setting out towards the market for the upaadhane. I too felt like going to the market with him. I went a few steps with him, but ran back home.

'Amma, Amma, give me a bag. I'm going to the market with Doddappa to beg for alms,' I said. She brought a bag and hung it over my left elbow. I followed my uncle towards the market.

We stopped at every house and said, 'Shriman Narayana Govindaaa, Govinda.' People put handfuls of flour, rice or wheat into the chombu. Some put money too. I crept to a side to take out the money and shove it into the pocket of my shorts. We also stood in front of vegetable vendors and said, 'Shriman Narayana Govindaaa, Govinda.' They gave us some vegetables.

'We've eaten. Go elsewhere,' said some people, giving us nothing. Suddenly, I lost Doddappa. I guessed my way back home. I placed the chombu and the bag in the hall and bowed to them.

I sat cross-legged at the door of the Durgammathaayi temple, engrossed in cleaning the coins I had pilfered. I pulled them out from the pocket of my shorts one by one, blew on them, wiped them clean with my shirt and put them into the pocket. Naani sidled up to me. He was amazed to see Lakshmi, the Goddess of wealth, dancing in my shirt pocket—jun, jana, jana. He suggested that we should hire a bicycle. He took me to a cycle shop in Narasimharaja Colony and got me a small cycle on hire. He got one for himself too. Both of us cycled to our hearts' content in the maidan of the Vidyapeeta Educational Institutions in Hanumanthanagara until we were utterly spent. Then we returned the cycles, paid the hire and walked back home.

Until I passed the seventh grade, I went to the market area for upadhane during Shravana Saturdays. I stole the money I got from begging and spent it on hiring a bicycle. That is how I learnt to cycle.

We never ever went to the Vokkaliga houses in the village near our settlement. When Doddappa was a boy, he had gone once to one of their houses to beg for alms. He stood in front of a house and shouted, 'Shriman Narayana Govindaaa… Govinda.' Someone came outside, stared at him, went inside again, brought out a cane and thrashed him. The welts on his body did not heal even after a month.

We are not in trouble when we lie about our caste to strangers in the marketplace. And in the towns, we can live like anyone else among strangers. This is a basic truth I found out when I went for upaadhane in the market area during Shravana month Saturdays.

Dagger-wielding Byranna

Every morning, as soon as I wake up, I go to Karegutte to ease myself. That day, I removed my shorts and sat in the shelter of a boulder. A rabbit came towards me, hopping. I stood up and threw a pebble at it. It jumped once and disappeared.

'Could it be hiding among the shrubs?' I wondered, treading gingerly and looking all over like a hawk.

I saw Byranna, a thoti of the scavenger community in our colony. He was skinning a buffalo calf in a shallow pit. I stared at him, mesmerized. He looked up this way and that, and when he spotted me, he signalled to me. I went over.

'Here, hold this,' he ordered, pointing to its leg. He was skinning it from one side, deftly, delicately. I was amazed at his expertise. Some vultures gathered from nowhere and circled overhead, screaming keey keey. He looked up and cursed them, hurried through the skinning, dusted the skin, folded it and tucked it under his arm. He stabbed the tender carcass in three or four places and slit it open. Then, he wiped his knife on some grass and tucked it into his waist.

'Come on,' he said. Even as the two of us were coming out of the pit, four or five vultures swooped down screaming and, landing on the carcass, began to tear at the meat and eat it. I kept turning back to watch their excitement. Byranna had gone ahead of me a little distance.

'Le, what's there to see? Come on!' he scolded me, turning back. I took a few steps. Thorns pierced my right foot. One of them stuck in it and broke off. I was pulling it out when Byranna came up to me and said, 'Take,' as he handed me a four-anna bit. I stared at it. It sparkled. I held it tight in my right hand until I reached home and put it away safely on a shelf.

'What a nice man! That Byranna gave me four annas!' I kept repeating to myself; I kept remembering Byranna.

The sun set and night came on. I had my dinner of ragi ball and stretched out to sleep. Then I remembered the four-anna bit. I reached up to it on the shelf and fingered it and curled up again to sleep. I had not yet closed my eyes.

'Will Byranna skin another buffalo calf tomorrow? Will he give me another four-anna bit tomorrow?' I kept talking to myself until a deep sleep overpowered me somehow.

The cawing of crows the next morning woke me up. I sat up straight. I rubbed my eyes and ran towards Karegutte. My mind was full of Byranna. I did not see him in the pit. The buffaloes and their calves were wandering about everywhere. I was disappointed. I ran up a big boulder and sat down. I looked around everywhere, but did not see Byranna.

The womenfolk with metal pots in hand sat between boulders or between shrubs for a while. They went their way, covering their heads with the pallu of their saris. They were staring at me as they went. I stood about for a while and then dropped down on my haunches. I did this over and over again. But there was no sign of Byranna. I got worried.

'You son of a thief! You're such a kid and yet you've learnt to do such things, have you?' Somehow, Thimmakka had managed to get close to me without my being aware of her. She was now holding on to my arm and was screwing my ear.

'Ayyoyyo!' I shouted. By then, Huchamma came up to us, tossing up tiny pebbles in her hand.

'Akkayya, take these. Twist his ear tight enough to lift his head. Then he'll see the Nandi Hills,' she said, teaching her a way of refining the torture. I bit Thimmakka's hand and ran from there.

Byranna was coming up the cart track with a buffalo calf on his shoulder. On seeing him, I stopped in my tracks. I kept staring with an eager longing at the dead calf.

'Come on.'

'Thank God, I'm sure of a coin today,' I said to myself, putting my footsteps in his. I looked up at the sun from time to time, praying, 'Swami, bless me.' I slapped my cheeks in penance. Byranna walked towards the boulder that we children used as the sliding board. He laid the calf down and lit a bit of a beedi and began to smoke—ooof, ooof. A wheeze became a rasping cough and bothered him.

'What did you do with the money I gave you?' he asked, wiping the sweat off his face with his shirt.

'I'm saving it, Anno,' I was in my element.

'Ayyo, you poor idiot! Instead of spending it on fried peanuts and other snacks, you're still keeping it, are you?' I did not know what to say.

He pulled out a knife from his waist and whetted it on a stone. He ran the thumb of his right hand along the blade. He sharpened it again. Then he slit the throat of the calf. Blood gushed out and made a red pool. He stuck the knife into the neck and dragged it down, slitting open the front from neck to stomach and a little below it. As he peeled off the skin, the sun glistened on its delicate flesh.

'Here, hold this,' said Byranna.

With great excitement, I stood holding the leg. Looking at the eyes and the skinned body, I felt sad for the calf.

'Anno, it's a tiny calf, isn't it?' I asked, 'Paapa, poor thing!' Suddenly, he pointed the knife towards my belly, that Byranna.

'D'you see this? How's it?' he asked. The knife flashed like lightning in the sunlight. Byranna's eyes shone like lamps. I could not speak a word. I held on to the leg of the carcass and stood still; I was that scared. The sun pierced my skin, bringing out beads of sweat.

'Will this Byranna give me money today too? If he does, how much will he give? Or will he not give at all?' Desire and greed struggled with possible disappointment within me.

Even as I watched, Byranna skinned the calf, dusted the skin, folded it and tucked it under his arm. He lit a beedi and, smoking it, took out a four-anna bit from his shirt pocket. 'Here,' he said, putting it into my hand, and walked away briskly. I touched the coin to my eyes and ran to my house without stopping anywhere on the way. I put it away with the other one on the shelf. Now I had eight annas. 'How much will I have if Byranna continues to give me money this way?' I wondered, but could not figure it out.

The midday sun had just begun to tilt a bit. Byranna was staggering down the Karegutte path. He was trying to sing, but he could not mouth the words. I was scared to see him. I slunk away from beside his house and ran away; I did not want him to spot me.

Suddenly, I heard the sounds of a brawl—crying and screaming. People had collected in front of Thimmakka's house. I stood at a little distance. Byranna had caught hold of Thimmakka by the top half of her sari and bent her nearly double. He could barely stand; he was doddering so much. Thimmakka had scratched his face with a short besom. It was red and bleeding. People rushed into the fray, got hold of them and pushed them apart. Byranna sat by his door, lolling about against the wall and stammering. I could not bear to look at his plight.

'Le, you nameless one!' Thimmakka was raging at him. 'Slog like the rest of us and eat! Then I'll call you an honest man. Drain the sweat of your body on Bhuthaayi before you eat! You hide fresh quicklime in the pocket of your shorts even before the first light of dawn. You stick it to the bum of the tender calves, poor things, and you slink away as if you haven't done a thing. By the time you come this way again, they are dead, poor creatures. Then, like a decent man, you come and skin them, sell the skin and try to twirl your moustache among the womenfolk, do you? Your moustache is only as good as my pubic hair, do you know that, you worthless fellow? You're taking the lives of dumb animals, you gutless thief. But remember this; your lineage will disappear without a trace…' Thimmakka kept cursing him.

Old and withered Malakkajji had heard enough. She could bear this ranting no longer. Slowly, she dragged herself towards Thimmakka, plucked the besom from her hand and tossed it aside.

'*The sin of the doer is in the mouth of the speaker*, goes the saying. Get inside,' she advised her.

I ran home. I put my hand into the shelf. The coins were still there. I sat down in the room. The words Thimmakka said to

Byranna echoed in my heart. Quickly, I took out the two coins from the shelf and tried to put them among the wicks in the lamp stand. I could not reach it. I laid two pillows on the floor, one on the other. I stood on them, put both the coins into the cup of the lamp and brought my palms together in reverence.

From that day, I did not even look towards Karegutte. If ever I happened to see Byranna's shadow, I ran away to escape from him.

My Father, the Eye Doctor

Quite often, fine splinters of chaff or stone got into the eyes of people working at the threshing floor or in stone quarries. Whenever this happened, our people suffered untold torture. At such times, they came looking for Appa to have it removed. Sometimes, they came in the evening after work; they would not let him sleep. They sat by the door chatting on topics like caring and concern, intimacy born of trust, rains and crops, hot and cold weather, the village fair and God, while they munched on betel leaves and nuts spiked with a pinch of quicklime.

At the break of dawn, Appa would go outside to search for a type of grass called garke hullu. He looked for the not-too-tender, not-too-dry kind with the leaves far apart…He bent the stem to see if it was supple enough to bend, but not break.

Turning the man with the splinter towards the morning sun, Appa sat on his haunches in front of him and angled the patient's forehead with his left hand.

'Where is it hurting?' he asked.

Then he gently held the eyelid open, pushed the rainbow-shaped stem of the garke soppu into the eye and removed the offending body with a snap—tachaar. Sometimes, no one could see it; it was that tiny. After a while, relieved smiles danced on the patients' faces. They brought their palms together gratefully. Some of them tried to touch Appa's feet. He jumped away, as if a snake had touched him. He would bring his palms together in return and mutter, 'To God, to God.' If they gave him money, Appa touched it to his eyes and tucked it safely away.

Appa was a reticent person. If ever anyone spoke to him at home, he replied with a crisp, 'Yes…', 'No…', or 'Really…?' Not a word more. He worked all the time like a dumb bull. Whenever he was free, he leant against a wall or a tree and snoozed as if he were meditating. People who saw him in that pose said, 'This Muthanna must be a yogi.' Appa never performed any puja; he only burnt incense to the ancestors on Marnomi during Dasara. He never bathed; he had to be forced to bathe on festive days. He was not depressed during bad times or happy during good times. I have never seen Appa laughing. He always wore a smile like Buddha.

Once, when I was threshing paddy at Thappateyappa's threshing floor, a bit of husk got stuck in my right eye and I could not open it. I felt as if the pain was sucking away my life. The husk was pressing on the eye the whole night through. Amma fed me a ragi ball, helped me drink water and, rocking me on her lap, told me a story, hoping to put me to sleep:

Once upon a time there was a village. Beyond the track to the village, lived an old cobbler of the Madiga community. He sat by the wayside and repaired the slippers of the passers-by. He received whatever they gave him if at all they did. But he never failed to ask them, 'Will you, by any chance, be going to Kashi, Swami?'

One day, someone important was getting his slippers repaired.

'Are you going to Kashi, Swami?'

'Yes,' the man replied.

'Then you must do me a favour, Swami,' said the cobbler, bringing his palms together, 'I've given my daughter in marriage in Kashi. I'll give you a packet of turmeric and kumkum. Hand it over to her as from her thavarumane, her mother's house, please Swami. You'll be blessed.'

'Give it to me,' said the man. The cobbler handed over a packet of turmeric and vermilion powders together with some betel leaves and areca nuts and brought his palms together respectfully.

'What's your daughter's name? Where does she live?' asked the man.

'She's everywhere in Kashi, Swami. You just have to say, "Amma, see, your thavarumane has sent you arshna and kumkum," and she will come and take them from you.'

'Listen, Ayya. What's her name? Where does she live? Tell me,' the man persisted.

'The Ganga that flows in Kashi is my daughter, Swami. Just go to the flowing river and say, "Here, Amma, your family has sent you arshna-kumkum. Here, take it."' The cobbler repeated the same request.

And so, the man took the auspicious powders and the betel leaves and nuts as a blessing from her mother's home to the daughter, Gangamma in Kashi, and went on his way.

While he was wandering about in Kashi, the man remembered the cobbler and his gift to his daughter. He had it tucked away in his pocket. Thinking that he would test the cobbler, he went to the bank of the river and said, 'Gangamma, look here. Your mother's family has sent you arashna-kumkum. Come and take it.' Immediately, Gangamma rose from the waters and stretched out her cupped hands. A bangle sparkled on each hand. The great man stared at the bangles as he handed over the auspicious gift. And even as Gangamma was disappearing slowly into the water, he pulled out a bangle from one hand.

He went to the market street in Kashi and tried to sell it. The traders took one look at the beauty of the bangle and said, 'We can't afford to buy it.' As the old man went about trying to sell it, he entered a kingdom. While he was trying to sell the bangle there, the king's courtiers caught hold of him and took him to the king.

'Where did you get this bangle?' asked the king. The man told him the whole story. But the king did not believe him.

'Fine. Arrest him and that cobbler and check them out,' he commanded.

The courtiers dragged the man all the way to where the cobbler sat by the wayside. He was repairing a slipper.

'What, Ayya?' said the courtiers to the cobbler, 'Is it true that you have given your daughter in marriage in Kashi?'

'Yes, Swami,' replied the cobbler.

'Is your daughter's name Gangamma?'

'Yes, Mahaswami.' The courtiers took out the glistening bangle and showing it to him asked, 'Is this your daughter's bangle?' 'Yes, Swami! Yes!'

'Come on then. Let's go to Kashi. Let's see if this matches the other one on her wrist.' They hurried him.

'Swami,' the cobbler pleaded, 'I came all this way only to go to Kashi. But, what can I do? I've become old and feeble. And so I've stopped by the wayside to repair slippers. Have pity on an old man and let me be. I'll fall at your feet.'

But the king's courtiers had no pity on the old cobbler.

'Well, all you need is a proof that this bangle belongs to my daughter, don't you? Is it okay if I show you the other bangle right here?' The courtiers were willing to see the other bangle of the pair. There was water in the mud pot used for wetting the leather to soften it for repair. The cobbler stirred the water thrice with a potsherd, brought his palms together before it and saying, 'Amma Gangamma, they want to see the other bangle of the pair. Give it to me for a moment. I'll show it to them and give it back to you,' he put his hand into the pot and brought out a bangle, as lustrous as the other one. From that day onwards, the grove beside which the cobbler sat by the wayside is known as Madiga's Grove.

Amma finished her story, but how could sleep enter an aching eye? Somehow, I managed to wait until dawn. Appa made me sit facing the sun and took out the fleck of husk from my eye. It did not sting any more, but it did feel a little sore for about two days.

The Ajji of the Dung-cakes

Our colony was in Thappateyappa's farm, between Kathriguppe and Kallasandra. Appa farmed Thappateyappa's son Ramanna's farm on lease. Two streams, Chennammakere and Kaneerkatte, joined at the tank near Thappateyappa's farm. Appa, Amma, Akka and Maava have suffered untold miseries to bring about the merger of the two streams into the tank that had once been dry.

I too worked on the farm during Saturdays when I had half-day school and on Sundays and other holidays. Attached to the farm where we worked was a hillock. The villagers from Kallasandra grazed their cattle, sheep and goats in that field.

An old woman from somewhere wandered about the field, collecting the dung and patting it flat like pancakes to dry on a boulder next to the farm. She turned them over after two days to dry on the other side. After another two days, the feeble ajji dragged herself about the field gathering the dung-cakes into a basket and disappeared among the crevices in the boulders. Perhaps she sold the dung-cakes as fuel. I thought of her as Beraniajji, the ajji of the dung-cakes.

Sometimes, Ajji crossed the fence to drink water from the pond in the farm. Patting some water on her head, she untied a little bundle at one end of the pallu of her sari to share the fried peanuts and peas tucked into it.

'Enu, Mari? How're you? Have you eaten?' She always asked me.

'Ajji, have *you* eaten?' I asked her one day. She sighed.

'I have to support the life in this body with some ganji or some greens, shouldn't I, Mari? Isn't that why I'm struggling this way? If God takes me while I'm still able to get about and fend for myself, I'll be grateful. I've have no one to look after me if I'm to sit in a corner. Even now, I've hardly anything to eat; it's a life without any money. I'll become a carcass with no one to call my own.' Ajji teared up as she spoke. I could not quite understand the story behind her tears. But I felt a twinge in my guts, an 'ayyo, Paapa, poor Beraniajji!' kind of concern for her.

If a week went by without seeing her, I craved her company.

One day, Ajji was standing on one of the boulders, waving her hands and calling out to me. I jumped the fence and skipped towards her.

'Careful! Careful! Look where you're walking!' she shouted. I reached the boulder and climbed it.

'Sit down,' she said. I sat. She untied the bundle at the edge of her sari and gave me fried green peas.

'Why weren't you here yesterday, Mari?' she asked me. She always called me her little one.

'I'd gone hunting.'

'Oho! Did you catch a tiger or a mouse?'

Both of us fell about laughing. Her face was wrinkled, her cheeks hollow. There was no life in her eyes. Her mouth revealed teeth as red as red mud when she laughed. Ajji always had a strip of cloth tied around her face. In it were some dried leaves. Once in a while, if ever she untied the cloth and spread it out, I could see strands of reddish hair.

One day, Venkateshappa and I were going to Yediyur to have horseshoes fitted for his bullocks. We met Beraniajji on the way. She laughed all the way as she took us to a house where tiles used to be sold. It may have been during her father's time or her grandfather's time. Dilapidated by sun, wind and rain, it looked like a bare-boned cow now, patched in places. The walls, weary of standing, had cracked. Bandicoots had dug holes in the yard, and some wild trees gave the place the semblance of a forest.

My shadow was under my feet. My throat felt hoarse.

'Ajji, I'm thirsty,' I said.

'Hoon, hold your palms together,' she said, bringing a metal pot of water. I cupped my palms to my mouth and bent a little. Water gurgled into my hands from above—jola, jola. I drank my fill. Right in front of me, Venkateshappa was drinking water from a tumbler. And then, he went inside and sat in Ajji's house; he was a Gowda. I sat out in the yard. The ground was afire with the blazing midday sun. My shorts was torn at the seat. I kept shuffling about like a cat with singed paws. I sat on my haunches for a while and stood up to shift my feet. I had stepped on thorns that very morning and my foot was throbbing. Caught between the searing sun above and the scorching earth below, I could not handle the heat. My eyes and nose were burning. My eyes were blur red with sweat streaming down from my head. And my head was splitting. The heat could have melted iron; it was that hot.

'In just a little while, you can eat your fill, Mari,' Ajji kept saying every time she came outside with the blowpipe in hand, rubbing her eyes. I was soaked in sweat. Ajji brought a bowlful of rice topped with spicy chutney and garnished with mustard seeds. She placed it before me. I ate a mouthful. It was tastier than whatever they call nectar. I ate it all up. The more I ate, the more I hankered for. Ajji kept serving me more and more, though I did protest. I sat on my haunches and ate. I could not squat on the seething ground. Suddenly, there was a gust of wind. The rice was covered with a fine coat of dust. My teeth protested, as the grit hurt them with each bite. Somehow, I swallowed the food, fearing that Ajji might say something if I wasted it. Ajji poured water. I washed my hands and cupped them for a drink. The water went the wrong way and I had a fit of coughing. Immediately, Ajji patted the top of my head.

'Look upwards at the sky. Look upwards, Mari,' she kept saying.

Venkateshappa stepped outside.

'Come, let's get going,' he said. The bullocks, wearied by the sun, were drooling as they chewed the cud.

'Ei, Mari! Ei, Mari! Wait, wait!' We had walked some distance when we heard Ajji calling out to me. She was coming towards us with giant strides, huffing and puffing. As soon as she reached me, she undid the knot at one end of the pallu of her sari and took out a four-anna bit and gave it to me. Her mouth was too breathless to speak, but her eyes spoke from her heart. She straightened my hair ruffled by the breeze.

'Go now, Mari,' she said fondly. She did not move from that place until we were out of sight. Though I walked on with Venkateshappa, my heart stayed back with Ajji.

I remember her every time I eat rice with chutney.

Friendships such as this
Have no stench of caste.
They have only
The bonds that bind.

Khaki Shorts and White Shirt

Our village is just one among thousands. On the outskirts of our village is the Aithayya Madhigara Hatti, a colony for Madigas, the tanner-cobbler community. In that colony lived a couple with their five Pandava sons and a daughter for a blessing. My parents did not know the comforts of the gentle morning breeze, of shade, of water. To swim across the sea of family life, they slogged on other people's farms and fields, sweating water and blood, overcoming hundreds of odds day after day, not seeing the snake that bit them or the thief that hit them until they became like besoms of dry twigs. As the years went by, even as they yellowed like leaves, even as their children grew wings, they held their hunger taut like bent bows and went hunting for food before break of day for any kind of work they could find and returned home only when stars twinkled with laughter in the sky. Even before their joys and sorrows, their anxieties and worries could find expression, their fatigue overwhelmed them, robbing them of their half-spoken words.

We could see the sun, moon and stars from inside the hut. Countless rats carried on their family life in the torn thatched roof. Their kiyon-piyon added to the soothing sounds of the wind and the stream, though they fought ferociously at times like the people in our settlement.

Our house was a banyan tree during the monsoon. Just as melodious notes from musical instruments mingle with voices to make an orchestra, the rhythmic thot thot sounds of rainwater dripping at varying pitch into different metal pots blended to provide sweet music to our ears. Quite often, Appa and Amma came home weary, unable to carry their exhaustion. Then Amma took a rag, mopped up the water from the floor, wrung it into a pot and poured it outside before going with a coconut shell from house to house to get some embers. She cleared the fireplace of ash, set the embers in it and arranged firewood over them and blew on them to light a fire to cook a meal. As she blew—oof, oof—into the fire, she also coughed—kuhu, kuhu. Tired of coughing, she put her head in her hands and prayed, 'Put an end to this worthless life, O Bhagavanthaa!' Wiping dry the wet grinding stone, she knocked the handles in place, put some ragi into the mouth of the stone, brought her palms together prayerfully and sang as she ground the millet into flour. The lilt of her song and the hunger in our bellies helped us to doze off. We woke up bleary-eyed, when she roused us to eat the ragi and drink half a chombu of water and lie down wherever we were, however we were. Appa and Amma would get hold of a hand and a leg and drag us on to mats woven with toddy palms. Thanks to the bedbugs, lice and mosquitoes, we slept fitfully, scratching ourselves all through the night until the first round of cock-crowing around three in the morning. We could drift off peacefully only around the second round an hour later, and we hardly heard the cocks crow again at five. As the sun rose, the bugs left us to clamber up the walls, glistening and heavy with our blood. We squished them, one by one.

Knocked about here and there, my son was shaped into a grinding stone, so goes the saying. Even so, I grew up playing games with the boys of our colony, hunting rats and birds, catching fish and crabs, eating wild fruits like dates and custard apple, and going around with farmhands who grazed cattle, sheep and goats. My baby talk made way for fluency, but my runny nose lingered. Amma cleaned other people's bathrooms and pleased them enough to beg for clothes for us. To us, those worn-out shorts and shirts were silk brocade. We wore them and paraded all over the colony, prancing and laughing with the sheer joy of having clothes to flaunt.

Once, when Appa and Amma had gone to work to fill our bellies, someone got me admitted to the village school. That school was in the area where the Gowdas lived. Sometimes, when the old teacher did not come, a new teacher gathered all the students together inside the closed porch of the Marammathaayi temple, but we had to sit outside. With the blessed sun staring at us relentlessly, our minds and bodies shrivelled up. When it rained, we raced home.

Somehow, I managed to enter the third grade. We had a Brahmin master. Most of his head was tonsured, leaving a tuft of hair at the back. He made us Madigas sit in a row behind the Gowda students. He had two canes to punish us, a short one to punish those children of the agricultural caste and a long one to reach us in the back row. Quite often, the zing of the cane, as it landed on our tender skin, nicked off a bit of flesh and left us bleeding and, later, scarred. He would not let us anywhere near the black board like the previous teacher. When he gave us dictation, he would not touch our slates. We had to place our slates on the floor and stand a little away. He ground his teeth as he looked at them and then hit us with the long cane. I passed the fourth grade and went to the Government Boys' Middle School, Basavanagudi. It is in one corner of the Krishna Rao Park. Our class teacher was Kamala Madam. We referred to her as KSK Madam. She was like the rain, wind and sunlight; she brought me goodies to eat sometimes.

Once, there was a memo: *Students are required to get khaki shorts and white shirts within two weeks. They should participate in the drill on Saturdays without fail.* I told Appa and Amma about it. A month went by, two months went by. There was no way my parents could afford to get me a pair of khaki shorts and a white shirt. The drill master Shrinivasaiah, who was also our English teacher, slapped me every Saturday for not being in uniform. I showed my parents my swollen cheeks and wept.

'Then, don't go to school, Maga. If you have life, you can somehow survive by selling salt at least,' Amma comforted me. That khaki chaddi and white shirt put paid to my studies.

Nanja of our village had told me how he had stolen a gold-coloured shirt from the dhobi ghat. That thought kept haunting me wherever I sat, whatever I did. I decided to steal a pair of khaki shorts and a white shirt and went towards the dhobi ghat near the Chinnamma tank for two to three days in a row, lying in ambush among the shrubs between the boulders. I could not see a single pair of khaki shorts. White shirts, lying on shrubs and boulders, dazzled the eye, but they were too big for me. I gave up the idea of stealing.

The python of hunger was swallowing us slowly, bit by bit. Amma and Appa were at their wits' end. They sent me away to Nanjappa Gowda's house to work as a labourer. Every morning, as the cocks crowed in the backyard—kokkakaa…

ko—I felt as if something had fallen on my head and woke up bit by bit. If anyone grunted, 'What is this, lazybones? How long are you sleeping?' I sat up with a shock, as if I had felt a whiplash. I brought my palms together praying, 'Swami paramathma!', slapped my cheeks in a ritual of penitence and got up, turning on to my right side for luck. I imagined the lilt in Amma's tender voice, 'Get up, Maga. You'll be late for school, won't you? You have to walk a long way, don't you? Turn to your right side and get up. Look at the picture of the deity…' and my grief flowed out as tears. I folded my torn blanket, put it away in the loft, tied the cattle outside the barn and swept it clean, piling the dung in a corner and filling the mud pot with urine and pouring it outside. When I carried basketfuls of dung on my head to toss it outside, I felt my neck grow shorter. My throat was hoarse. My feet stumbled. The urine from the dung in the basket trickled down my face, tickling my nose and my mouth. When I cut grass from the meadow and brought it in, the sweat streamed down to my legs.

With tears in my heart, I watched the boys from our colony in white shirts and khaki shorts with bag on shoulder and books in hand, laughing their way to school.

I had worked on the farm for daily wages for twenty-five days. One day, I chopped my left thumb while cutting grass in the meadow and the blood marked my footsteps all the way to the village. That day, we had a heavy downpour. I was drenched to the skin and shivering. 'Ayyayamma! Ayyayappa!' I kept groaning. A calf in the barn mourned with me, 'Ambaaa! Ambaaa!' The Gowda's wife grew tired of scolding me and threatening me.

'Go, get lost! Come early tomorrow morning,' she said and sent me packing. I raced home in one breath like a caged bird soaring towards the sky.

Our neighbours ground some herbal greens and bandaged my thumb with the paste. The fever rose as the day waned. I was ill for about ten days. As I was recovering, one morning Nagappa sent for me, 'Come back to work.'

'I won't,' I said, 'I'm going to school.' I ran away and hid in the Karegutte. The sun was right above me. I was hungry, my throat was dry. If that heartless Nagappa spotted me, I would be like a frog in a cobra's mouth. The more I thought of it, the more my head felt heavy. I dozed off. When I woke up, the rays of the sun were slanting. I slunk home stealthily like a cat.

I was manuring the tomato patch in Sunkenahalli Gowda's farm. I found a pen shining in a bag of manure bought from a store. Somehow, I did not have the heart to write on the palm with it. I wrote on the back of my hand. The writing was dull. I wrote my name on a piece of paper. The letters laughed like stars in the night sky. My classmate Muniswami was walking back from school, happy in his khaki shorts and white shirt.

'Have you left school, Lachma?' he asked me.

'No, Muniya, I'll come back next year,' I said.

'But you have a pen ready already?' he teased, laughing. I felt as if the basket of manure on my head was laughing at me. I wept.

That night, I had a sweet dream. I was in uniform, khaki shorts and white shirt. My hair was oiled and combed. I was walking to school with that Muniswami. I was in the drill with the other boys. I was playing kabadi, knocking down two boys with one stroke. I opened my eyes happily, but it was dark.

'Amma!' I shouted in fear.

'Why, Maga? What happened?' Amma asked flustered, as she woke up and lit the lamp. The light flickered and died as I narrated my dream to her.

'Maga, let your earnings be with that Sunkenahalli Gowda. We'll get a pair of khaki shorts and white shirt stitched for you in exchange. You go back to school,' she said.

I had worked for Gowda for three months. The school year commenced after the summer vacation. Gowda gave me a white shirt and a pair of khaki shorts that fitted his son. I put it on and went about everywhere in the locality, announcing to everyone I met, 'I'm going to school tomorrow!'

Evening gave way to night. My stomach was full with just half a ragi ball. I touched my uniform from time to time. I could barely sleep that night. When I woke up once, it was still dark. I lay down again, but did not close my eyes. I woke up as the cocks crowed for the second time, brushed my teeth with charcoal powder, bathed in cold water, put on the khaki shorts and white shirt, stood in front of Durgammathaayi temple with my palms together and put some of the kumkum from the threshold on my forehead. By then, the whole colony was aglow with morning light.

My classmates were now in the next higher class. As soon as she saw me, KSK Madam's face bloomed like a jasmine. The red gulmohar flowers were laughing like my heart. I wrote with my new pen in my new notebook.

I Join the Narasimharaja Hostel

My home in Kathriguppe was three miles from the Old Fort High School, next to Tipu Sultan's summer palace in Bengaluru. I had seen people travelling in the Government Road Transport buses, but I had never been in one. Many of the students studying with me commuted on these buses, but it was my plight to walk.

Whenever my friends said, 'Come, let's take a bus,' I felt strangled. I was ashamed of my poverty.

'I don't have the money,' I said, head bowed.

If they bought something to eat during the tea break, I felt sad. I could eat some goodies only if they shared them with me.

I always sat in the last row. I sat quiet for, what with hunger and thirst, I had no energy to talk. The boys in my class were smart and sprightly. They were good at games and lessons. They were fooling around all the time, teasing one another and laughing. I alone sat with a long face. I was embarrassed by my clothes when I saw the smart ones the other students and teachers wore, all crisp and pressed.

'You don't have enough to eat. You don't have enough to cover yourself. Why do you need to study? Come on!' said a voice inside me.

'Okay, I give up school, let's say. What kind of a job will I get then?' countered another voice. Tossed back and forth in this dilemma, I became like a broomstick.

Most of my classmates were not friendly with me. My only friends were V Basavaraju, Guruprasad, Mahadeva and Jagadish; Jagadish because he was from our colony and the rest because they were Dalits. As soon as the bell rang for lunch break, the students ran outside like birds flying from the nest. I went out, drank water to fill my belly and came back to my place and lay my head on my stack of books and tried to catch a nap, but I never could.

Every Thursday, we had games during the second period. When my classmates played, I watched them while keeping watch over their books. I too wanted to play with them, but my hunger and weakness held me back.

One of my classmates was Raghavendra from Begur near Nelamangala. During lunch break, he sat in a corner of the class after the others had left. Facing the wall, he gobbled up his food. He never talked to me. If ever anyone touched his lunchbox, he did not eat his lunch that day. He would toss the food away immediately, right in front of our eyes! 'O, God! How *I* could've filled my tummy with it if only I could've had it,' I said to myself. Some four or five boys in our class teased Raghavendra mercilessly. Deliberately, they tried to touch his lunchbox. He held on to it tightly and ran about the room. They laughed at him as they chased him. I sometimes could not help giggling. There was trouble in the class only because of that Raghavendra. Once, even the headmaster Shri Seshagiri Bhatt came to the class to speak to him.

'Don't tease this boy,' he warned the others.

One day, Guruprasad came dancing his way into the class, singing a film song during lunch break. I sat up immediately.

'Ei, why're you sleeping? Why don't you talk to the others? Why don't you join in the games?' he asked. I did not raise my head.

'Come, let's go to the hostel,' he said, dragging me outside. I followed him to the hostel like his pet. He made me sit on a steel trunk and went somewhere. The room was full of pictures; pictures of gods and film stars. Guruprasad returned with a plate in each hand, singing a film song. Each plate had a ragi ball and some curry. Both of us ate well. He went back with the same plates and brought back some rice and curry in each. The curry smelt good.

'Join the hostel, Lachma,' he said after we had eaten.

'Okay,' I said. He took me to our class teacher, MS Madam.

'Madam, I'm getting him admitted to the hostel. I need his conduct and caste certificates,' he said. She wrote out the certificates immediately and got them signed by the headmaster. I tucked them away safely in the Kannada textbook, as if they were rubies. After the second period on Saturday morning, Guruprasad asked MS Madam for permission to miss the rest of the classes for the day. We walked all the way to the office of the Department of Social Welfare. I handed over the certificates to an officer, repeating what Guruprasad had taught me to say, parrot-fashion, 'I have to join the hostel. Please grant me permission.' The officer ran his eyes over me from top to toe.

'I'll send you to the Yelahanka hostel. Go,' he said.

'Saar, but he's studying in Fort High School,' Guruprasad butted in. The hostel warden happened to be sitting right there.

'Poor boy, Saar! He looks poor. He's come barefoot. Give him admission to our hostel,' he pleaded on my behalf. The officer wrote something on the sheets of paper I had given him. The warden took them, saying to me, 'Come to the hostel tomorrow.'

I went home and told Amma and Appa. I also told them about the ragi ball and rice I had eaten three days earlier.

'They serve us snacks like uppittu and chitranna for breakfast, and we can eat all we want for lunch and dinner. We get soap and oil as well,' I said, explaining to them the benefits of being in a hostel.

'That God has saved you from walking three miles on a hungry stomach. That's all that matters, Lachma,' said Amma, raising her palms together to the sky. The news spread everywhere in the colony, reaching even Ramanna, my younger elder brother, working for the chairman of the village.

I brought out the metal trunk that Venkataramanappa, my eldest brother, had got for his wedding. I soaked it in water and scrubbed it with a strip of coir. Sweat poured from me, but I could not make out the original colour of the trunk. Jayarangamma, my elder sister, watched my struggle while cleaning the greens. She went inside, brought out a cake of washing soap and handed it to me saying, 'Here, take this, Lachma. Rub it down with this soap.'

As I scrubbed the trunk with soap and water, grime and grease flowed out to show up the original green trunk with orange stripes.

'Abba, now my self-respect is safe!' I said to myself and let it out to dry in the sun. Then, I packed all my books in it. I folded the bed sheet that Vokkaliga Venkateshappa had given me and put it in. My heart was filled with peace and with some good resolutions: 'God has saved me from worrying about hunger. Now I must study well. I must get a government job. I must keep Appa and Amma from working as farmhands.'

Early the next morning, I washed my face, carried the trunk, stopped at the temple to pay my obeisance to Durgammathaayi and went about the settlement wishing everyone goodbye. Bylamma sat at her door, combing her daughter's hair.

'Ayyo, look at this!' she said, 'Those who go to that place are orphans. Poor boy, he has everyone, and yet they are sending him there because they can't feed him.'

'Is that true? Are all the boys in the hostel orphans?' asked a voice in my head.

'Oh, let that be. How many days will you live without food?' comforted that same voice.

My eldest brother came home. He gave me eight annas. I bid my family goodbye.

'Jopaana, Maga, be careful,' Amma advised me, 'You say that boys from places we don't know and haven't heard of will be there with you. Don't get into trouble with any of them. Don't fight back if anyone says anything. Keep quiet. Don't interfere with anyone.'

I set out on the road towards the City Market. I felt sad to leave my birthplace, my parents, relatives, friends and the people from my colony. But the hostel enticed me with the promise of good food and schooling without any anxiety.

A new world! I entered a new world with new experiences and continued my studies in a new way, perhaps. I had no worry about food, but whenever I ate, I could not help but remember that hunger still stalked my family at home. Though food in the hostel was tasty and clean, I could not eat much. I had known hunger since birth, and so my belly had shrunk. I felt full with a little food. Children much younger than me ate much more than I did. It took me a year in the hostel to eat a normal quantity.

I bathed every day. There was a red champak tree near the hostel. I picked the flowers and offered them to the gods as my worship. The temple of our family God Venkataramanaswami was right next to the hostel. I circumambulated the temple every morning on my way to school.

One day, after going round the temple thrice, when I sat meditating on God, I remembered something that left a bad taste in my mouth: One year, on the Yugaadhi festival, Chikkanna finished his work at the chairman's house, came home and had the ritual oil bath for the New Year, rubbing his body down with oil and standing in sunlight for a while before washing it off with soap-nut powder and steaming hot water. He smeared the three lines of caste-marks on his forehead, put on the new pair of shorts and the shirt that Patela had given him, threw a new towel over his shoulder, packed the puja items in a bag and set off towards the Krishnarajendra Market to worship our family god in the temple near the market. Our worship at home would not be complete until he performed the puja in the temple and brought home the tirtha, the sacred water. That was the rule, a ritual. When Chikkanna was on the bus to the City Market, someone picked his pocket. He had no money to pay for the puja at the temple, no money to offer when the pujari brought the mangalaarathi plate around with the sacred lamp, no money even to take the bus home. He had to walk all the way back home. He came spent and sad after the day was done and darkness had settled in for the night.

And now, I lived right next to the Venkataramanaswami temple. Not a day went by without a dot of kumkum from the temple on my forehead, without the akshathe of rice grains on my head or a flower from the prasad stuck behind my ear. I had filled out and my face had a glow. I wore pressed clothes. The very classmates who used to ignore me previously spoke to me now. Every Thursday, we had an hour for games. The film actor Shakthi Prasad supervised our games. I enjoyed myself playing, debating and joking with my classmates.

Though I am a Kannadiga and I speak Kannada, I spoke in the variety of the language that we Madigas speak, and I spoke it with a sense of self-worth. The children at school laughed at me and teased me. Once, when we were talking about ragi, I used the expression naatiragi for the millet. Then, one of the boys said, 'Not means no. Does that mean he's talking about some ragi that doesn't exist?' All of them laughed. They were not aware that I was referring to the seedlings set aside to be transplanted. From that day onwards, I spent less time with my friends and more with my books.*

I strutted about our colony in my NCC outfit; boots, khaki shorts and shirt, cap with red plume and an NCC belt. I was better than any sepoy as I marched about—left, right, left…Dust swirled at my feet and rose to mingle with the breeze as I did an about-turn. I was the king of kings, marching down the street.

Once, Kencha from the Holeya settlement was coming my way. As soon as he spotted me, he bent his head and walked away, pretending not to have seen me. He was barefoot in the sizzling sun. The towel on his head was torn. His belly peeped out in places from his torn shirt, his shorts were dirty. We had been close friends in the fourth grade. I ran to him and stood in front of him, barring his way.

---

* The boy is teasing Lakshman, punning on naati, which means the ragi (meant to be planted) and naat, which is his pronunciation of 'not'. Only those who have heard 'not' mispronounced as 'naat' may catch the joke.

'Le, Kencha,' I said, 'What's this? You're running away from me as if you haven't seen me. Why? What wrong have I done to you?' He had faint traces of a beard and moustache now. His eyes had lost their shine. His cheeks were sunken. Poor Kencha. He stopped going to school and worked at odd jobs as a coolie.

'You're all dressed up smartly, Lachma. And so I was scared to talk to you.' We opened out to each other and talked for a long while. Memories of the sweet childhood we shared soothed us like a healing balm.

As I was leaving, I put out my hand and said, 'Shake hands.' He did not understand what I was saying; what I meant. I drew out his right hand, clasped it firmly and shook hands with him. He was laughing as I went on my way.

The people in our colony hesitated to speak to me. The people from the village saw me from a distance, but would not come near to talk to me. Then I realized the impact of education. Wealth, authority, knowledge and their trappings mesmerize the ignorant, filling them with fear.

A Wedding Feast that Cost Me My Government Job

Knocked about here and there, my son was shaped into a grinding stone, so goes a saying.

I too finally made it to the State Board SSLC examination, overcoming countless difficulties, insults, hunger and thirst. But I failed in English.

Anjanayya from our settlement used to wander about the marketplace and read the daily news. One day, he brought me the Kannada daily *Kannada Prabha* and said, 'You've studied up to SSLC. The law, says this job, is reserved for Dalit candidates. Apply for it.' I typed an application and posted it to the address mentioned in the advertisement.

Within a month, I was called for an interview for the post of a peon and watchman from Balaji Vidyaniketan Shri Kumaraswami Vidyamandira. I showed the letter to Anjanayya.

'Look, you'll surely get the job. Annayappa, the chairman of our village and the secretary of the school are good friends. Show this letter to the chairman,' he said.

When will the sun set? When will darkness appear? When will my elder brother come home? When will I show him this letter? My mind was so filled with eagerness that I forgot to be hungry. 'Once I get the government job, our hunger, poverty and all other difficulties will be burnt,' I said to myself.

The goddess of sleep sat in my eyes and made me dodder like a drunkard. My brother came home around the time people without any worries complete a cycle of sleep. I showed him the interview letter and repeated to him all that Anjanayya had said.

Even as the cock crowed, my mother, elder brother and I were on our way towards the village. Darkness covered the sleeping land like Karidevva, the black demon.

My brother and mother set about cleaning the cattle shed belonging to the chairman's household; tethering the cattle outside, sweeping the shed, carrying loads of dung on their heads to the garbage pit and emptying bucket loads of urine into the drain.

My eyes were weary with peering into the darkness. After a long time, the dusky eastern sky reddened like the laughter of a freshly blooming red hibiscus. Beams of sunlight were eager to reach the earth. Crows cawed, sparrows twittered. I thrilled to their sweet voices. The cool breeze soothed my body and mind, as the shade of a honge tree refreshes someone exhausted after slogging in the blazing sun. 'Shouldn't the wind have fragrance?' I wondered even as my mind sang:

The land that has no sun has no radiance
The life that has no education has no value.

The sun was laughing in the east. I stared at the rising orb. I felt there was nothing to match its beauty.

'Oho, our boy has come to ask for something,' said the chairman, as he came outside after a long while. My mother's voice, mingled with fear and shyness, stuck in her throat. Immediately, I handed him the letter calling me for an interview.

'I'll tell Naidu,' he said after reading it.

Annayyappa is like a brimful vessel; never noisy, never one to panic. I have never seen or heard of him beat or scold anyone. Ramanna, the younger of my elder brothers, has worked for his household since he was a boy. He said that the Patela had neither spoken to him roughly nor lifted his five fingers even once to slap him.

On the day of the interview, I bathed, brought my palms together in obeisance to the threshold of the temple of Goddess Durgammathaayi, lit joss sticks to the photos of the gods in my house, prayed to them and went to the interview like a devotee to a temple, announcing the good news to everyone I met on the way.

The person conducting the interview was shimmering in crisp clothes. He was laughing too. I was trembling; my throat went dry. He asked for my name and where I was from. He checked my serial number and caste certificate and said I could go.

Some twenty to twenty-five days later, the postman brought me a letter in mid-afternoon. It said I had to report for duty with my original certificates within a week. My dreams took wing and flew to the skies to touch and talk to Chandrama, the moon, and the stars; I was that excited.

No one in our community had ever got a government job. Everyone in my family rejoiced with me. I vowed I would get pujas performed to our family gods with my first salary.

Narayanappa, a clerk, received my original certificates and he himself wrote out my letter reporting for duty. I signed it. I began my tenure as a government employee like a bride stepping into her husband's house for the first time, with eagerness, joy, fear and shyness. I won the love and trust of every employee at Kumaraswami Vidyamandira. One of my duties was to bring lunch for the headmaster from his house.

Nagarajayya, a peon, seemed a very mild person with sacred ash on his forehead, a flower on his ear and a linga of Shiva on his neck to proclaim that he was a Lingayat. But he spouted foul language whenever he opened his mouth. I heard that backbiting was second nature to him; he created misunderstandings and quarrels in the school. Even the headmaster and the teachers were uneasy with him, fearing that he would carry tales about them to the secretary. Everyone had a thus-far-and-no-further kind of relationship with Nagarajayya. No one trusted him.

'You have to be friendly with him and yet wary. Understand?' the headmaster had warned me.

Nagarajayya would bring eatables, coffee and tea for the staff from a nearby restaurant and pocket the tip, smiling strangely. He would make me wash the dirty glasses. Once, in one or two months, the board meeting would be conducted in the school. Nagarajayya and I would get the room ready, dusting, sweeping and swabbing the room and arranging the furniture. He would serve refreshments during the meeting and make me clear the table and wash the plates and glasses.

'Look here! When you walk about in the secretary's presence, remove your slippers, fold your arms respectfully, remove your ring and watch and put them in your pocket,' he would say. I did as I was told.

'You'll have to be the night watchman at school, Secretary's orders,' said the headmaster to me one day. His face looked like a wilted flower.

I was scared of spending the night alone in the school premises. I would take Ramakrishna from our locality and teach him until we were sleepy. And yet, I was nervous throughout the night. Once, in the dead of night, the Gurkha watchman came around blowing his whistle. Though I was afraid, I ventured out as he was familiar to me. He could speak Kannada fluently, better than many Kannadigas, though it was not his mother tongue.

'Where's Nagarajayya?' he asked.

'The headmaster has said that I have to be here at night. Nagarajayya will take over during the day,' I replied. He face fell.

'Ayyo, you haven't yet sprouted a moustache!' he said and sat down with his hands on his head to recover. 'Okay, go and sleep now,' he said and went on his beat, blowing his whistle and beating his lathi on the ground. At daybreak, the Gurkha came again with a police whistle, gave it to me and said, 'Here, blow this whistle once every hour. If there are any thieves lurking around, they'll run away.' His eyes were laughing. I treasured the whistle like a precious ruby.

A stray dog used to sleep at night by the compound wall in the backyard. I would feed it a bun every night. It would come to me wagging its tail as soon as it spied me from wherever it was and whine kui kui, speaking to me in its language. But at the slightest sound, it would bark—bow, bow. The whistle from the Gurkha and the dog gave me the strength of a hundred elephants. I forgot my fear of darkness.

To the hungry, even spoilt food is like a festive meal, they say.

Even so to me, the night duty or day duty did not make a difference. Whatever it was, it was a government job, wasn't it? On the first of every month, I received my salary. People from my slum and our relatives developed affection, respect and an intimacy with me for no reason at all. The elders often asked me for small change to buy betel leaves, areca nuts and tobacco to chew and beedis to smoke. I gave it to them. They touched the money to their eyes and blessed me, 'May God bless you! May you live in peace!' They pestered me for months on end, reminding me to pay for the toddy to celebrate festivals like Yugaadi and Mahanavami festivities. And when I gave them money, they got drunk and praised me.

The secretary of the school, M C Naidu, celebrated the wedding of his son. He had invited the staff to the wedding feast he hosted after the ceremony. His son was at the entrance, bringing his palms together respectfully and shaking hands with the guests welcoming them. I was eating in the secretary's house along with the other guests as he came along.

'Namaskar, Saar,' wished the secretary like a gracious host.

I wished him back with due respect.

Immediately, he looked shocked as if he had stepped on a snake. He seethed with fury, breathed heavily and stared at me as if he would swallow me. His dark face grew darker.

He came to the school that very night.

'Namaskar, Saar,' I said, bringing my palms together reverently.

'Your work is at night. Why were you in the school during the day?' he roared. I could not look at his face; it spewed evil.

'The headmaster told me to, Saar. He himself brought me to the lunch in your house, Saar.'

He blew out his cheeks, cleared his throat noisily and spat. Then he went away, mumbling something like a pujari muttering a mantra.

'A person with no smile on his face, no warmth in his words isn't human at all; let him be,' I felt.

As usual, I went to the school the next evening. The headmaster looked depressed.

'Don't come over to my house from tomorrow,' he said. 'Just see to your work at school. Here, take this letter. Read it and reply to it.'

It said:

> *The labourers working on the new building have been using the wood meant for scaffolding as firewood for cooking and you have done nothing about it. This has resulted in loss for the organization. You do not patrol the area. You sleep in a room instead. The Secretary has taken note of this personally. Hence, why should not action be taken against you? Reply in writing within three days of receipt of this letter.*

I was bewildered. I felt as if life was oozing out of me; my hands and feet were trembling. The words in the letter seemed to stare at me like an ogress. The headmaster looked worried, and Narayanappa, the clerk, looked down at his feet, as if he was counting his toes. The three of us were silent. After a long while, the headmaster laid a letter on the table. It had a lot of writing on it.

'Sign here,' he said. His voice was gentle. I signed.

Narayanappa walked out of the room suddenly with tears in his eyes.

'What next?' Anxiety bore into me, as a drill bores through a piece of wood.

That M C Naidu spat every time he set his eyes on me. He stared at me from toe to head. He assigned duties to me unnecessarily. He seemed like an assassin to me. Every time I saw his shadow, heard his name or imagined his face, I felt a sinking in my heart. I did not mind if no one brought his palms together to salute me. But I told myself, I should live in such a way that no one should fear me.

A week later, I went as usual to sign in the attendance register on the headmaster's table. 'Don't sign. The secretary's orders. Hand over the bunch of keys to Nagarajjaye,' the headmaster said, head bowed.

I could not comprehend the mystery in this situation. Everyone locked up the premises and left in a hurry, as if they feared the building would collapse on their heads if they lingered any longer. Nagarajjaya was closing the gate.

'The secretary will be coming; one thing may lead to another. Go, go, go home,' he said and went inside.

'Why was I asked not to sign the register?' I wondered, as I stood outside the gate. 'Why have they taken the keys from me? They're asking me to go home. Does that mean they don't want me to work here any longer? What wrong did I do that I shouldn't have done?' I found no answers. Someone seemed to be clutching at my life; my head felt heavy.

The countless white flowers on the jasmine creeper that had climbed on the arch over the gate used to glitter in the light of the street lamp. Their scent permeated the air, bringing me great joy. I would have a cold water bath in the mornings and pick some flowers and worship at the Ganesha and Murugan temples. I would circumambulate the navagrahas. But that day, the jasmines appeared to wilt. The dahlias seemed to be crying. I looked at the flowerbeds, remembering that I used to water them regularly; the soil was damp. I was tired of standing there. The dog too stood beside me. It was around nine at night. I got on my bicycle. And suddenly, the dog began to moan. The faster I rode, the louder I could hear the dog's cry. The moaning of the dog mingled with the way I was sent away from my job; my grief overwhelmed me and my mind was in turmoil. The headlamp of my cycle brightened a path, driving away the blanket of darkness that covered the land. Though I cycled with all my energy, the bicycle moved forward with the tread of an elephant.

My mother was surprised and very happy to see me.

'Come, come,' she said, 'How long it is since you were home at night! Come, pour some water on your hands.' My parents looked at my face in the light of the lamp.

'Why are you looking strange? What happened?' they asked anxiously. I told them of the injustice and deceit. Everyone was worried. Our home became a house without light. Fear danced on every face. Everyone was dumb with dread. No one could think of a way out.

'Let it be as God gives,' my mother said after a long while. Her words gave me courage like a flash of lightning brightening the dark world.

After three days, Nagarajayya came home with an injunction: The secretary wanted me in school by ten o'clock the next morning. He left abruptly as soon as he had delivered the message.

'What's awaiting me now, O God?' I wondered as I went to school with much apprehension.

Nagarajayya grinned artificially and disappeared. A brief smile flickered on the lips of the headmaster, Narayanappa and the other members of the staff. Looking this way and that, they shook my hand or waved at me to show they were glad to see me and became engrossed in their duties.

'Lakshman, you're like a son to me, Ayya,' said the headmaster, taking me beyond the gate and putting his arm over my shoulder, 'Whether a thorn falls on a banana leaf or a banana leaf falls on a thorn, it's only the banana leaf that will get hurt. You've anyway got through the SSLC exam. If not this job, you'll surely get a much better one. Let the two of us go to the DDPI's office. You'll have to sign a paper there. If you don't, no one can touch you here, but I can guarantee that the secretary will organize a theft at night and blame it on you. Then, what will you do? Can we be watchful of deceit? To begin with, your family is poor; why do you want to ruin your life? Their duplicity will destroy them; let them be. Mark my words, God will surely bless you.'

We went to the DDPI's office in Kalasipalya, Bengaluru. The headmaster and the DDPI spoke to each other in English in low tones, while I stood in front of the officer. He placed a sheet of paper on the table and asked me to sign it. Something was written on it. Everything the headmaster had told me was protesting within me. The baleful face of the secretary seemed to appear before me.

I signed the paper.

'Don't go to the school henceforth,' said the DDPI. I felt a fire in my belly. 'Ayyo! Ayyo!' my mind screamed. Tears streamed from my eyes.

'Swami, we're poor,' I pleaded, embracing the feet of the officer. 'Trusting in this job, we've taken a loan from the Patela for my elder brother's wedding, Swami.' I beat at my breast and wept. Some men like Yamadharmaraya caught me by the neck and pushed me outside. After a while, I went back to the DDPI's chamber and spoke to him, bringing my palms together as one may yearn to speak to a corpse, 'Swamy! Swamy!'

'Hand him over to the police!' thundered the DDPI.

The headmaster put his arm over my shoulder and took me out of the room. The silence of the sky descended to the earth to envelop us. My distress had plucked my words from my mouth. We stood a long while under a tree, like the tree. Hunger, thirst and sunlight were too scared to touch us. The headmaster put four one-hundred rupee notes in my hand, covered his face and wept.

'May our relationship remain this way forever! Come home whenever you can,' he said, wiping his eyes with his handkerchief and stroking my head. Then, he disappeared from sight even as a piece of ice melts in the sun.

Nagaraja, a member of the teaching staff, spoke to the assistant secretary of the organization about the injustice done to me. He sent for me to meet him in his house and said, 'Take a few people with you and see the DDPI and the Minister for Education and tell them about the unfair treatment meted out to you. You'll get back your job.' I had no one to help me. I could not meet anyone.

It is only after I joined the Dalit Sangarsha Samiti in its struggle for justice and wandered through villages meeting other Dalits, whose lives were on the streets like mine due to the malice of caste distinctions, that I realized why I had landed a government job in the first place; what it implied when I sat among the other guests at the lunch arranged by the bridegroom's family and, ultimately, why I had lost my job through no fault of mine.

I understood why people of the upper castes do not permit Dalits to enter their homes, wells, hotels and temples; the problem was larger than what had happened to me as a person. I read the writings of Ambedkar, Periyar Ramaswami and the revolutionary, Basavanna. I got involved in the protests of the Samiti and experienced both victory and defeat.

Undying Love

I had not passed the High School SSLC examination, but the strength of my desire to enter college grew like a huge tree; I decided I would work if need be and continue my education and some day get a government job.

A few boys from our locality went to Bengaluru to work as painters. They looked smart in their shirts and trousers! I too went with them as a painter.

'If anyone asks you which caste you belong to, you must say you're a Vokkaliga without thinking twice.' That was the first lesson I learnt on the painting job.

It was not scary to paint new houses. We would walk around the house freely, singing as we went about our work. But embarrassment and fear plagued us as we worked on old houses. The residents grimaced at the way we looked. They watched us keenly at midday as we went out for lunch, and in the evenings as we finished for the day and went home. This made us feel ashamed. We suffered in silence.

If we had a job for about a week in one corner of Bengaluru, we had another for a week or two in another corner of the city.

As I was new to the job, I was given sandpaper to scrape the doors and windows. I had to scrape the walls with sandpaper and dampen them before painting. I soon looked like a white demon. Within two months, I started a wheezing cough and spat sputum with lime dust. My skin became dry and wrinkled like brinjal burnt on coal fire. My hair turned multicoloured. Street dogs barked at me.

On Saturdays, when we received our weekly wages, my fellow workers drank, ate and saw a movie. Though they were always desperate and discontented, they had faith and fear in God. Whenever there was a problem or misfortune, they said, 'Who can be responsible for our fate?' They firmly believed that they were paying in this life for the sins of their previous birth.

If the sins I've committed are powerful,
What can anyone do to help, O Hari?

They sang to forget their pain. Though the painting jobs were strenuous, the money earned did not last till their doorstep. And so, the painters were disgruntled.

Was it because painting houses served merely a cosmetic purpose? Was it because it did not help anyone or contribute to any kind of social upliftment?

On Sundays, my mother heated a huge cauldron of water for my bath. I dipped a rag in kerosene oil and scrubbed my body with it. I removed the paint from my face and my hair, had a bath, put on clean clothes and went to Jagadish's house.

A family from Bengaluru belonging to the Devanga community of weavers had built a house about a kilometre from our settlement on land owned by someone in the city. Jagadish was from that house. We had studied together in the old Fort

High School. I attended school from the hostel, while he came from home. Since we were from the same place and in the same class, a deep friendship developed between us. Both of us had failed the SSLC exam. His parents praised me sincerely every time they saw me, 'Poor boy! See how hard he works. Such a good boy!' Jagadish and I sat under a tree in front of their house and read our lessons and wrote our assignments. Once in a way, we would see a movie in Hanumanthanagara.

Once Jagadish's mother said to me, 'Mari, get a castor leaf.' I plucked one. She served me four idlis and some chutney to go with it. I ate it. I cupped my palms and she poured water into it. I drank it. All the members of Jagadish's family were friendly with me.

When I got the government post of a peon and watchman at the Kumaraswami Vidyamandira, there was a special glow in our house. I was treated with unexpected respect and dignity. Denying myself food and clothes, I had saved enough to buy a bicycle. For more than a year after I got the job, I scrimped and saved. With the help of Earanna from our locality, I bought a gold ring set with white stones at a pawnbroker's in Basavangudi. I had become smart in the way I dressed and conducted myself.

I sat for the SSLC exam again and passed. I took laddus to Jagadish's family in celebration. We were like twins, he and I; we were never separated, not even for a day.

A little beyond Jagadish's house was the house of an overseer of construction workers. His family and Jagadish's father were like the snake and mongoose; they could not stand each other. Jagadish's father was very short-tempered.

Jagadish's elder sister Kamal had failed the SSLC exam. Sometimes, she discussed the lessons with me. We had become friendly. Once, when her mother had served me some snacks like uppittu and kajjaya on a castor leaf, Kamala had asked, 'Amma, why do you serve him on a leaf? Why don't you serve him on a plate?'

'Tell me, Mari,' said her mother to me, 'Can we give up caste distinctions just because you happen to be a good boy?' I bowed my head.

One afternoon, I went to Jagadish's house. Kamala was doing something in the backyard.

'Is Jagadish at home?'

'He's gone to my grandmother's house. Why didn't you come here for over a week? You got through your High School, anyway. But I haven't; however hard I studied. Get into a college and study well. But what'll you do with the government job you have when you join college?' Touched by her sincere concern, I replied to her with great respect and walked away home.

'That Madiga, Lachma, and your daughter spend hours on end talking and giggling,' complained one of the overseer's household to Kamala's mother, sowing seeds of suspicion in her. It reached Kamala's father and he, in a moment of insanity, beat her with a crowbar. Kamala's head had bled, but, for whatever reason, he had not taken her to the doctor.

'I'm taking my sister to a doctor in Hanumanthanagara. Come over there,' said Jagadish to me, explaining the situation.

I was bewildered. The more I thought about the issue, the more confusing it seemed. I could not pinpoint her crime and the punishment meted out for it. My gut wrenched; I found myself sighing from time to time.

'Ayyo Paapa! Poor thing!' I kept saying to myself. I got on my cycle and it sped like a plane in the wind. I rang the bell as I cycled away—tring, tring. My clothes were soaked in sweat.

People and vehicles on the street seemed to whizz by. Whenever drops of sweat dimmed my eyes, I wiped them away.

Jagadish was sitting in front of the clinic. The pain in his heart spread over his face. I could not speak due to grief and exhaustion. My mind was in turmoil.

'Wipe your face,' Jagadish said.

The lady doctor called me in. She had dressed the wound on Kamala's head and bandaged it. She had heard from Kamala all about how she had got hurt.

'Do you love her?' The doctor asked me. I started trembling. My heart raced. I felt I was falling deep into the earth, reaching the netherworld. 'How can it be that this doctoramma talks as if she's making the earth and heaven as one?' I felt. I was tongue-tied.

'Ayyo, what a situation! All because she spoke to me as a friend,' I was weeping in my heart.

'What, Kamala, do you love this man?'

'Doctoramma, he's a very good boy. My family respects him and I've approved of him.' Kamala's voice was like music to my ears. Her heartfelt sentiments stirred me. They filled my heart to the brim. My throat went dry and my eyes filled.

The lady doctor laid a hand on each of our heads and blessed us. 'Be brave, both of you. Get married to each other for love; don't fear anyone. I too married for love. May God bless you!'

Jagadish and I continued to meet and talk as usual. This incident did not ruin the intimacy between us even a little. I did not look towards Jagadish's house even through the corner of my eye. The wound on Kamala's head was nothing when compared to the wound in my heart.

'Ei, Kamala, why did you go and talk to him knowing he's a Madiga?' asked Kamala's mother one day, as her head was healing, 'What was there that you should talk to him? Look, all this furore, this Ramayana, is because of him.'

'Amma, haven't you and Appa told us many times that he shouldn't have been born in that caste? That he's a good boy? What's wrong in talking to such a good boy?' Kamala retaliated.

Jagadish reported the conversation to me that very night at the school where I was working. It got me wondering, 'What was the cause of the misunderstanding between the overseer's family and Jagadish's father? What is it to their family if Kamala and I talk to each other? Did we say something we shouldn't have? Or do something we ought not to do?' I was in an anguish, thinking of the doctor's blessings, the intimate concern with which Kamala had spoken to me and of her suffering a gash on her head for merely talking to me. I felt perplexed.

Without my being aware of it, I developed love for her; respect and caring. I thought of her all the time, whether I was sitting, standing or dreaming. I hardly had peace of mind.

'My akka wanted me to give this to you,' said Kamala's little sister one day, handing me a love letter and a red rose. My heart thrilled to her baby-way of speaking. The sweet face of the little girl, her dulcet voice and her smart walk brought me great joy as often as I remembered her. But the more I stared at the letter and the red rose, the more nervous I became.

I waited for the street to be empty before I stood under a tree and opened the note furtively. Suddenly, someone rode past on a motorbike. I got scared. I hid it quickly and walked to another street. I looked around and saw no one. I opened the letter again slowly. 'I'll come to the school where you work at two this afternoon,' it read, 'I feel like seeing you, talking to you. Don't misunderstand me, Your Kamala.'

I put the red rose into the pocket of my shirt, as if it were a gift, a prasad from God, and the letter as if it were a precious ruby and peeped into the pocket from time to time. The oftener I read the letter, the more I wanted to read it. Happiness, anxiety and fear clashed in me, making me tremble all over. 'Two o'clock, two o'clock…,' I was saying to myself. I felt as if I was standing on thorns. I kept looking at my watch every other moment. Every minute seemed like a year.

When I was younger, whenever there was a slight drizzle with sunshine, we used to dance and sing with joy:

The sunshine and rain are coming together
The crow and the fox will wed each other

The happiness that filled my heart now was much greater than that. I stammered when someone spoke to me. As I walked to a shop reading the letter, I almost dashed into a girl walking towards me. When I looked up, the girl was smiling gently. For a moment, I mistook her for Kamala. Whatever I was doing at work in the school, my eyes were glued to the gate. As two o'clock neared, my heart began to beat faster. Exactly at two, Kamala's sister was at the gate! I felt a tightness in my chest. Looking this way and that, I walked quickly towards her.

'Akka's calling you.' I thrilled to that little one's charming voice. Kamala was standing farther away. I lifted my head and looked at her hesitantly with shyness and fear. Her face looked like that of Goddess Saraswati Devi in pictures. She stood with her head bent. I too stood beside her with my head bent. I do not know for how long we stood that way.

'I'll go,' she said at last, offering me a box of sweetmeats.

'Hm,' was all I could say. Countless words remained with me, unspoken. From that day onwards, my beloved was like a whirlwind holding me, body and soul, whatever else I was doing; standing, sitting or sleeping.

Another day, Kamala's sister came near the school and handed me a steel tiffin carrier and a handkerchief and walked away without a word. The carrier contained a sweet delicacy, payasam. And two parrots were embroidered on the handkerchief. Below one bird was embroidered in threads of varied hues, *Lakshman*, and below the other, *Kamala.* Kamala had poured out her very heart into her skill in needlework. My craze for her grew and I lost the need for food, water and sleep. Day and night, I sang love songs from movies.

Before the wedding invitations were to be distributed for my younger-elder brother Ramanna's wedding, my family smeared auspicious red kumkum and yellow turmeric powders on the corners of the cards, placed them in front of the pictures of gods and did puja for them to be blessed. I stole one of them, scored out the name of the bridegroom and wrote *Lakshman* instead and similarly replaced the name of the bride with *Kamala* and sent it on to Kamala as a loving wedding invitation. I got an inscription painted on my bicycle: *Na ninna mareyalaare.* It was the opening line of a popular Kannada film song and meant, 'I can't forget you.'

One day, I met Kamala unexpectedly at the kadalekai parse, a groundnut fair in Basavanagudi. We prayed to the Doddabasavanna, the bull, hewn out of a single rock, 'Swami, please don't ever separate us, Swami!' We vowed before the god that if ever anyone hindered our unison in love, we would embrace and drown in a river to be ever united in death. I was unable to sleep if I could not see her even for a day. I would stand, staring at the sky every now and then. I would see Kamala's form in the drifting clouds and would thrill to it. And even as I watched, I would see the clouds break away, leaving me disheartened.

Kamala's father somehow got to know of our hearts throbbing with love. He spoke about it to M C Naidu, the secretary of the Education Society of the school where I worked. That man could not bear to see me in good clothes. He would scold me for no reason, screwing up his face the moment he saw me. He made me work like a bull tethered to an oil press. Though there were ayahs in the primary school, he made me clean the rooms and toilets. M C Naidu and Kamala's father snatched away my government job from me. After losing my government job, I was like a lonely dove.

Kamala would not eat or drink; she washed her hands in tears. She also feared for my life. She secretly sent me love letters. I too sent her love letters. These letters became our food and drink, and the very air we breathed. She had gifted me a gold ring with a white stone as an offering of her love.

One evening, Kamala came to the house of Seenanna, a Vokkaliga family of farmers, where I conducted night classes. She wept helplessly. I could not console her. Though we had been in love for two summers, and though I had been alone with her quite often, I had never touched her. When I saw her in tears now, I could not control my anguish; I wiped the tears. Her cheek was as soft as a fluff of cotton.

'I won't go home. You lost your government job because of me. I'm going to stay with you,' she bewailed.

'Meshtre, come what may, we're here for you,' Seenanna of the Vokkaliga community said. He addressed me as teacher, giving me courage. 'Don't let down the girl who loves you.'

Gowramma, Seenanna's wife, put a red dot of kumkum on Kamala's forehead and flowers in her hair, and on my forehead she put the mixture of vermilion and turmeric powder kept by the picture of the gods and blessed us, 'May you live happily for a hundred years!' Her wishes bolstered me with the power of a hundred elephants. In the enveloping darkness, I walked away from my town and my parents and relatives, holding the hand of my beloved. I felt there was no joy compared to the happiness of being with your loved one. We walked towards the house of a friend in Jayanagar with glow-worms lighting our way across thorns and stones.

A few days later, my friend T R Baati and some of his relatives and our friends got together and got us married according to the tradition at the Satyanarayanaswami Temple near Sajjan Rao circle. With great gladness amid the chanting of mantras by purohits, I tied the thaali round Kamala's neck at the temple, signifying that I had married her according to traditional rituals. Such a thing can happen in a city where purohits do not know our caste; they are happy with the dakshina of a hundred rupees.

Our friendship, respect and love for each other made us man and wife. And that love became immortal. As a witness to our love, we have three precious children—Gowtham, Jaibheem and Samathaavaani.

Towards the Light

I was barely sprouting a moustache and beard around that time. Some of the upper-caste Reddis from Maragondanahalli in Hoskote taluk had killed a Holeya of that locality by kicking him and bashing him with building blocks of stone. Why? He had refused to remove the carcass of a cow from the village.

The Dalit Sangarsha Samiti that fought for the rights and privileges of Dalits planned to stage a protest march against this injustice. My friend M Basavaraju compelled me to join him. And so I went along with the crowd, holding a torch aloft and shouting the slogans the organizers taught us, parrot-fashion. I walked barefoot over stones and thorns, climbing hills and dunes. The protest songs we sang to the beat of drums helped us forget hunger and thirst.

The sun tilted towards the west. The procession wound its way on the ruts of a cart track beyond a water tank. To the right was a wall of eucalyptus trees. Our songs of struggle stunned the earth and the sky into silence in this remote place. We walked our weary way with the drums beating in tune with our grief, anger and humiliation. The hillocks liked our songs of suffering and the accompanying drumbeats; they echoed their appreciation and support. The trees in the groves danced to the tunes, swaying in the breeze. The gentle breeze became cooler, showing us the true spirit of selflessness. From time to time, the guajalakkis set up a raucous chatter in the trees, egging on our voices with their killekyaako, killekyako…They sounded much like the way we shout to encourage one another while sacrificing a buffalo or a kid to God during the village festival—killellele-kyaako, killellele kyaako! Other birds too sang their songs tirelessly and tunefully to the tunes in their own languages, like poets revelling in their new creations. Cranes flew overhead, one tailing the other in the sky, with no restrictions on where they go, with no doubts about who they are. They were flying towards some country somewhere in the world, flying with ease and grace. They were a pleasure to watch as we trudged along the dusty cart track.

All of a sudden, out of nowhere, some twenty to twenty-five rakshasas jumped out of a tractor and fell upon us like armed highway robbers waylaying travellers. They looked like armed mercenaries trying to save the crown of some king somewhere, while they hardly had anything to cover themselves. The Dalit friends who had joined us from in and around Hoskote ran helter-skelter. The police who had followed us at a distance in their van turned a blind eye to the situation, indicating their silent assent to our plight. Had the power of khadi brought from them their sense of duty? Was there an order from a senior officer whirring about under their caps like a trapped cockroach? The police did not free anyone, did not arrest anyone. We gave a written complaint that Paramashivayya, the circle inspector of Hoskote taluk, should be suspended for dereliction of duty in not enforcing the law in the victimization and the murder of an innocent Dalit.

A fight ensued between those gundas and those of us from Bengaluru. Chiranjeevi Hebbala Venkatesh, a singer, was beaten unconscious. The police pretended to do their duty, screaming and shouting, just as we shoo away an eagle ineffectually, 'dhuuu, ya, dhuu', after it has swooped down on a brood of chicks and flown away with one and disappeared into the clouds. One of the gundas had come on a motorcycle. When a river snake and a cobra are entangled in love play and the cobra notices anyone watching them, it chases that person. A sensible man tosses a strip of cloth towards the snake and it spews its venom on it, presuming that it is the man. Similarly, we who had been victimized caught hold of that hapless motorcyclist and beat him up mercilessly and dumped him in a pit nearby. And then, we carried on with our protest march with torn banners and broken placards.

We held an open-air meeting in Hoskote, condemning the malicious attack of the rowdies and the studied indifference of the police. We petitioned that the hooligans be arrested, that Paramashivayya be suspended and that those who had unjustly killed the innocent Dalit with building blocks of stone be arrested for murder and tried as criminals.

It was around ten that night. We were standing outside the police station when a shower of stones was pelted at us. We were huddled into a police van and brought to Krishnarajapuram around one o'clock. I do not know how many of us would have lost our lives if we had to take the bus that night. We spent the rest of the night in front of R Muniyappa's house in the Dalit Colony, singing songs and discussing issues. Some of us slept in front of a few houses, wherever we could find some space.

Towards early in the morning when the sun was a huge ball of fire, we met together, planned our future protests and took the bus towards the city. From that day onwards, a desire sprouted in me to participate in as many forms of protest against injustice as possible.

It was around nine by the time I reached college. My clothes were crumpled; my hair and face were a sight.

'What is this? Did you work as a coolie the whole night through?' asked Shrimathi P K Umabai Madam. 'Is this any way to come to college? What will the other students think? Go, go immediately. Go and have a bath first,' she said, handing me a cake of Mysore Sandal soap. I went to the bathroom and had a bath in the tap water. I dusted my clothes and wore them.

'Now look at you! You look like a bridegroom!' she said, looking at me indulgently as an elder sister looks at her little brother.

I had been like the living dead. The songs of protest infused me with new life. Whether I was sitting or standing, the songs echoed in my ears. And I began to sing them to myself without embarrassment whenever I was alone. They pervaded my mind and created a forum for new ideas, new issues.

Whenever I interacted with people of the upper castes or developed a friendship with them, I met with new problems and faced fresh insults. But now that I had participated in the protests by the Samiti, I felt a new peace; a sense of self-worth I had never known before. I felt a new courage, a conviction that I was no longer an orphan. Here, I have presented you only with only a few pots of water from the vast sea of protest.

Though Dalits have been cultivating government land for ages, no vote-seeking political party had ever regularized the land. The Samiti decided that petitions to regularize the land in favour of the tillers should be presented at the offices of the tahsildars in every district and that strikes and lockouts should be arranged in front of the offices to press the demands.

M Venkataswami, the convener of the Samiti in Bengaluru district, sent me to Nelamangala a day before the lockout. Right then, the Samiti was burgeoning at Nelamangala. Dalits from the surrounding areas assembled in front of the tahsildar's office under the midday sun; thousands of hungry men in ragged clothes milling around like magpies. The police in khaki flashed their guns together with wielding their lathis. The whole of Nelamangala shuddered to the beat of drums and the slogans of protest. Yellowing leaves floated from trees. Ramappa from Harashinagunte talked to the police.

Siddalingaiah, N Murthy and I sat with sad faces and bent heads, leaning against the door of the office, as if we were not a part of what was happening. The police had moved towards where the action was. Slowly, I pulled out a lock from my pocket. A plainclothesman shot out from nowhere like an arrow from a bow. He landed on me and snatched the lock from my hand. The police took the three of us to a police station, abused and manhandled us.

The slogans of protest increased in tempo:

Dalit Sangarsha Samiti, zindabad!
Let the land of the Dalits be regularized.
Down with police excesses! Down! Down!
Long life to the solidarity of the poor in every caste!
Long life! Long life!

In response to the uproar, the faces of the police looked menacing, like those of people who had not eaten for many days. Suddenly, the clamour grew and the pushing and shoving increased. A senior police officer had arrived on the scene with a new convoy. They stuffed us into the Nelamangala police station. We filled it to overflowing, spreading out on the veranda too. They watched over us like fire-spewing dragons. They took down our names, the names of our parents and addresses. We had learnt a long time ago to give a wrong address when arrested. I gave a false name and a false address: Yeshwanthpur Dalit Colony, Bengaluru. A sub-inspector standing close to me guessed that I was lying. He looked at me from head to toe.

'House number?' he growled.

Immediately, G Muniraju from Yeshwanthpur shouted out a number that came to his head. The police officer who was taking down the information wrote down that number. Adiappa of Manjunathanagar began to giggle at the stupidity of the police. Seeing him, I could not control my laughter; I burst out laughing. The sub-inspector walked away, embarrassed.

They took our left-thumb impression in their police records of convicts.

'We're not convicts. We're protesters. We won't put our thumb impressions in your records.' However much we objected, it was no use.

'Yes, you're protestors. We'll need your thumb impression to give you an allowance.' A senior police officer told us a lie.

By then, it was around four in the evening. Many of the organizers had not yet washed their faces. People had to get back to distant villages. We were freed at five o'clock.

A chubby-cheeked little boy from a Dalit settlement in a village in a taluk in Doddaballapura (I forget the name), had grown up as a bonded labourer. He may have been bonded from birth to his master as repayment of debt owed by his father. The cattle, sheep and goats in the farm and the forest, the rice and ragi fields, trees and shrubs beyond it were his only relatives and friends. And now, the snot from his nose had made way for scraggy hair on his lips and chin.

The landlord of the farm had a grandson. He was the split image of the bonded labourer. The whole village was surprised. Poisoned tongues wagged on the striking resemblance between the two.

'If you plant a ridged gourd, will you get a bottle gourd?' they whispered behind his back. Could he be an illegitimate son of the landlord's daughter-in-law?

The landlord's grandson grew in body and mind.

Do you need a mirror to look at the wound on your palm? So goes a saying.

Once the boy realized that the proverb described his situation, it did not take him long to buy some five or six gundas by immersing them in a tub of liquor and warming their hands with thousands of currency notes that feature the non-violent Gandhithatha. They sharpened their knives to kill the labourer for no fault except that his master's grandson resembled him.

The ten corners of the world connived to carry out that heinous act. The whole earth gave silent assent to the Gowda's grandson's wicked plan, fearing his upper-caste status.

Who can tell if poison or milk courses in the veins of men? Who is to find out? Unaware that death was stalking him, the bonded labourer went about his work on the farm. The hired hooligans flogged him, kicked him and chopped off his head with a sickle and hid it in a gunny sack. They tied the headless body in another gunny sack, tied it with a rope to a stone slab seven feet long and drowned it in a tank beyond the village and relaxed.

One day, while farmhands, who generally swam in the tank after washing the cattle, were swimming in it, their feet touched the slab. They felt all over it and touched the rope. They were filled with fear, excitement and curiosity. The news spread through the Dalit settlement and the village, reaching right up to the Dodballapura Police Station and the ears of the activists of the Dalit Sangarsha Sangha.

At ten o'clock, M Venkataswami, Chinnaswami and I took the last bus from Bengaluru to Doddaballapura. We spent the whole night in a run-down house without food and with nothing to protect ourselves from the cold night air. We did not want either the police or the people of the upper castes to know we were there. We went to Katcheripalya and Veerabhadranapalya before the break of dawn, gathered the Dalit youth from these colonies and went on to the village where the innocent Dalit had been killed, and we had a secret meeting with the people of the colony.

Three days later, we organized a protest rally and an open-air meeting in Doddaballapura. We petitioned that the culprits should be arrested immediately and the family of the victim compensated. The film actor V Nagaraj spoke spiritedly at that meeting. His speech kindled a new hope and a new energy in the youth. People wept to hear the protest songs that Mavalli Shankar sang to the beat of his drum.

L Hanumanthaiah was of the same district. He described the condition of the Dalits in a moving manner.

Had I not known of the Samiti, I might have been a mercenary moneylender, perhaps, earning interest on interest, draining people's blood, seeing them bleed to death and saying, 'That's their fate; they're paying for the sins of their previous birth.' Or I might have become a political dissembler; the servant of servants pawning Dalits to a political party for political power, turning a blind eye to murder, extortion, rape and fraud. Or I might be wasting my life chanting mantras to Krishna or writing the countless names of Rama.

I can confidently say that I have been a self-respecting person with compassion for others, thanks to the Dalit Sangarsha Samiti.

Dalit Sangarsha Samiti, Then and Now

The communities of Dalits in Karnataka lived like dogs and foxes, enduring humiliation and injustice for centuries as if their lives were not worth living and their death was a sweet release. The awareness of their degrading situation and a sense of self-worth sprouted in the people when the Dalit Sangarsha Samiti came into existence.

As an organization, it empowered Dalits to protest against injustice as a community. It organized countless rallies against governments to fight for their rights and privileges. It fought also against such social evils as the caste system, the devadasi system, bonded labour and labour without recompense and also against the evils of drink. On the whole, the Samiti was like the rising sun, the dawn of a new beginning to the Dalit communities. Many of the organizers pledged that they refuse to be educated in the traditional system of education controlled by purohits that preached social inequality to favour the priestly class of Brahmins. They also vowed to give up drinking because it kept them, as a working class, in a drunken stupor by dulling their senses. The office-bearers became models of leadership. They arranged marriages between the Madigas and the Holeyas to break down caste distinctions between the two subsects and to bring about unity between the two communities of the lowest caste.

Jigani Shankar, a graduate, had married a mute girl on the dais set up to celebrate Ambedkar Jayanthi. M Ventkataswami, a bank manager, married a widow. The leaders of the Samiti became progressive in their ways. They became mountains of fire against injustice. They met with Dalit communities during Ambedkar Jayanthi celebrations and the inauguration of the branches of the Samiti and listened to their joys and sorrows. Such occasions resembled village fairs. They sought solutions and planned protests. Protest songs were composed as voices of the suffering communities. They gave up their settlements, their villages, relatives and friends and government employment and committed themselves to toil for the freedom of the Dalits. Kotagaanahalli Ramaih gave up a bank job to work for the betterment of his people. On the whole, the Samiti undermined the complacency of the government. It became the eyes and ears, the very breath of the exploited communities in Karnataka. It became their kalpavriksha, their Tree of Plenty.

But the dedicated band of Dalits of those days is not to be seen now. The protests of today are like coins with no currency value. Dalits have developed an attitude of compromise to serve their selfish ends. There are instances where some Dalit communities have been cheated and fleeced in the very name of the organization, in the name of other Dalits communities. Individual leadership has replaced group leadership. Slogans renting the air during strikes and protest rallies are not about victory to the Samiti, but to individuals. If truth be told, some of the members chopped down the kalpavriksha and auctioned it off to unethical politicians for power, for individual gain.

Today, atrocities against Dalits have multiplied. If the first plough has furrowed crookedly while plowing, is it fair to complain that the ploughs following it are not furrowing straight? The vanguard of the organization has to be prepared to endure troubles and losses naturally. Any social struggle is a bed of thorns, not of flowers. Our struggle lost its thrust at the hands of some timorous leaders. They satisfied themselves with parading the picture of Ambedkar in processions, forgetting that he was vehemently against personality cults. They forgot his philosophy; they forgot his vision of comprehensive betterment of Dalit communities. Once, when my friend Pattabhi and I were talking about the Samiti and the Dalit situation, he said, 'Saar. The office-bearers of the Samiti have made Ambedkar a blank cheque, Saar.' That statement is true, a hundred per cent true. Today we have organizers who have acquired property, wealth, cars, bungalows and government positions, all in the name of the struggles of the Samiti. It would not be wrong to say that they have been treacherous to Ambedkar and to the Dalit community. They have auctioned off the philosophy and tenets of the Samiti. Their struggle is to belong to the upper caste, upper class.

The activists of the Samiti have lost the ability to discern between friend and foe. They note the subsects among Dalits and discriminate between them, while appearing to protect the rights of the whole community. That is the reason the Madigas are fighting to be categorized as a scheduled caste to enjoy the benefits of reservations meant for that category. The Holeyas still live in the village, while the Madigas live in the colony.

When the Dalit Sangarsha Samiti was inclined to support the Janatha Dal political party, it was like noticing a well by day and falling into it at night. If any political party was for the people, would there have been any need for the Samiti? From this, it is obvious that the Samiti did not ever aim at a transformation in the lives of the Dalits; it only strove to improve their immediate social condition. Such a sea-change in the community as a whole is a matter of life and death. It cannot be a give-and-take transaction while siding with the exploiters.

There was a time when songs of protest were also songs of awareness:

'We haven't come for votes' they say,
'We haven't come to bribe with notes,
We are not compromising politicians.'
Thandhaani thaana, thandhaani tha
Thandhaani thaana, thandhaani tha
Here's a car coming for votes, Anno!
Take off your slipper and strike them in the face!

But today, the activists of the Samiti sing a different tune:

We've come to ask for your votes, Anno!
Not to bribe you with notes.
We have to compromise, Anno!
If we're to do politics.
Thandhaani thaana…

The activists of the Dalit Sangarsha Samiti descended to the level of walking the streets and singing such songs while begging for votes. Many of them lost their bearings with such wrong steps. They bartered the community aspirations of the Samiti for their personal status; for a smarter way of life, for wealth, for power. They joined different political parties and stood for elections only to bite the dust. Political posts for the Dalits do not imply some three and three-quarter Dalits getting to sit on the three-paise chairs in the Vidhana Soudha or in Parliament.

It involves a fight for the dignity of Dalits against such age-old social practices of inequality as caste-based segregation, daily-wage and bonded labour and the devadasi system. When this great vision of the Samiti crumbled, I and so many other activists like me had to desert it.

Once upon a time, there lived a wealthy man. He had an only son. Though the boy had grown up to be a young man, he did not have the slightest sense of responsibility; he was prodigal in his ways. The father was worried.

'What should I do now?' he said to himself, 'My son doesn't know how to manage my wealth sensibly. It will surely fall into the hands of strangers.' He then decided that his son should not get a single meal or a glass of water in his house.

'See, Magane,' he said like snapping a twig, 'You'll have to earn your own living. You'll have to pay for your board. Or else you won't get any food or water or shelter in this house. If you don't, you can go anywhere else in the world; just get out of my sight.'

The boy had never known such a situation; now he did not know how to face it. He went about begging people for work. He slogged the livelong day and brought home what little he earned and handed it over to his father every evening. One day, he had toiled hard from morning to evening. He was exhausted by the time he wended his way home. As he was about to hand over his wages, his father said, 'Throw it into the well.'

The boy was livid with fury. 'Appa, have you any sense?' he cried, 'I've broken my body since the morning to earn this and you're asking me to toss it into the well!'

Even so, the founding members in the frontline of the Dalit Sangarsha Samiti tried to straighten out the new members who had lost their sense of direction and misused the organization that the selfless visionaries had built up from the grass-roots level with their hunger, thirst and toil.

But society did not see us Dalits as human beings, though we served as the slaves of slaves, pleading with gods and religion for respite; though we lived truthfully, justly, dutifully and honestly.

Now there is only one question facing us: Should such inequality continue to survive? Should it grow? If those who do not have a life, anyway, do not come together to fight inequality, the untouchable in this country will continue to die every moment. Those who survive will have to live like slaves, worse than dogs, worse than foxes.

Once, there was a town. And in that town was a house. And in that house lived a man with two pets, a dog and a cat. The dog lay in perpetual wait for a chance to attack the cat. Though the cat grew in years, it did not grow in maturity; it continued to live in fear of the dog. And so, there was no way it could come out of the house and see the world outside. Why? Because the dog always lay by the door. One day, the dog went out quite unexpectedly. The cat was very happy. It walked about freely around the house. It felt like wandering out to see the world. It stepped beyond the threshold. It looked this way and that. It saw the town, people, animals, birds, shrubs, trees, water, shade, light…It was blown over by the beauty. It yearned to enjoy everything, experience everything. It walked down the main street with great dignity. It saw a mouse, hunted it down and ate it up. The cat was as happy as when it was given creamy milk at home.

The dog saw the cat sauntering down the street. It burned with fury. How dare it walk about independently with self-respect as if it were an equal! It wanted to get at the cat's throat and gulp down its lifeblood. The dog sprang towards the cat—chung, chung, chung. The cat saw the dog and began to run for its life, trembling.

'Today the dog will get me for sure,' it said to itself. But right then, palaar! A thought struck the cat; a thought that had never occurred before:

'Yes, from the moment I was born, I've laid the joy of being on my own at this dog's feet. I've eked out my life in fear. And now, there's a threat to my very survival. Fine! Anyway, I'm going to die. Let me face up to this wicked dog at least in my last moments. It has robbed me of happiness, peace and independence. I must kick it in the face with my left foot.'

The cat looked back. The dog was bounding towards it, baring its canines. The cat stopped in its tracks. Baring its teeth in a feral snarl and raising its forelegs menacingly, it stared at the dog with bloodshot eyes, gurr, gurr. The dog was stumped. It got scared.

'What's happening?' it thought, 'All these years, this cat would run at the very sight of me. But today, it's fixed me with a hideous glare. It's actually spoiling for a fight with me! Surely, this can't be a cat. This must be some other animal stronger than me.' And so, it ran away with its tail tucked between its legs.

The cat was now filled with a new sense of self-worth.

'By now, I would've been torn to bits by the dog. I myself would've sacrificed my life. But I saved it by protesting against the unfairness of it all. And so, if I have to save my life henceforth, I have to be ready to fight such mean dogs.'

From that moment, the cat lived happily. It lived for many years.

My Dalit friends, fellow victims of injustice, treachery and malice, what do we learn from this story? Just as there was no way the cat could have survived if it had thought even for a moment that it could not stand up for its rights against the dog, even so we have no chance of survival as long as we live in fear; however long we may live. On the other hand, if only we unite under revolutionary organizations and fight without compromising our principles, we can kick out inequality in our very lifetime. Or else, we ourselves would be supporting that inequality and injustice. We would be teaching future generations the same slavish mindset. Therefore, think. Would you live for generations as slaves? Or would you rather live in dignity for a day?

> *The country is extensive*
> *Time is eternal*
> *A dharmiya man, virtuous like me will surely come*
> *If not today, tomorrow…*
> *Some day.*
>
> —Bhavabhuthi

Like the words of the poet, countless revolutionary organizations are sprouting in Karnataka like shoots from the earth under the summer sun. They are thriving with new ideas and new perspectives, thanks to a sense of commitment to sacrifice in the members. However much the discriminatory system may try to quell the protests, it will be like holding up one's hand to block out the sun. These progressive organizations give sleepless nights to those against them; they wipe away the tears of the downtrodden. This is my firm belief.

The Caste Mindset Is a Mental Illness

Just as the fish need not be taught to swim, the untouchables in this country need not be taught to be humble, wary, religious, servile…

I was tired of life. I was tired of living in a village. I had suffered humiliation for no fault but that I belonged to a particular caste. The ritual pollution of my caste trailed me like a vicious serpent wherever I went, sat or stood. As a result, I developed a sense of low self-esteem; a feeling of helplessness, guilt and fear. I became depressed. I was a mental case.

The cruel practice of untouchability in the caste system was like a thorn in the sole of my foot, hurting me at every step. I lived like a trapped mouse, worse than a dog or a fox; as a slave of slaves, fed on injustice, hunger and humiliation.

It is impossible to say how many stones make a hillock. It is just as impossible to describe the disgrace and difficulties I endured for this one reason that I was a Madiga. I was so weighed down that I could not find a way out. I tried to find solace in being religious. I wrote down the name of Rama one thousand times. I bathed in cold water every morning before worshipping God. I observed the rituals of every festival diligently, at times borrowing money to fulfill my obligations. I fasted for Shivarathri and kept the vigil, the jagarne. I sent money as offerings in my name to temples in Dharmasthala and Tirupati. But I found no respite; I did not get even an iota of social justice or respect.

During one Shivarathi, I had fasted the whole day and kept vigil the whole night, singing bhajans to praise God. I had bathed in cold water the next morning. I had gone to the temple for the puja and worshipped the pictures of the family gods in the house before having my breakfast. I was sitting on the front porch of my house when Appa came with a flock of sheep. He had grazed them all the way from Dhonkalahalla and come towards Karegutte.

'I'll eat some hittina mudde. Keep an eye on the sheep,' he said, stepping into the house. While watching the sheep, I felt drowsy and stretched out on the stone platform in front of the house. Appa had his ball of ragi and came outside to see the sheep straying away. They had gone beyond Karegutte towards the Chennamma tank bund. Appa reached them and checked to find four of them missing.

'There's no end to your piety and puja,' Appa scolded me. 'Look, I've lost four sheep.' From that day onwards, he never sent me out to tend the sheep.

Whenever I suffered injustice, humiliation, misery or loss, my mind found a voice.

'If it is true that God is omnipresent and saves everyone from trouble,' it kept asking me, 'why is he tolerating the injustice meted out to me? I haven't done any wrong, but I'm being unjustly targeted for no reason at all day after day. If he is supposed to save the righteous and punish the evildoers, why is he allowing this to happen? What sins have I committed?'

Initially, I would voice these questions among my friends hesitantly, in fear, with despair, embarrassed that I should be talking this way at all. I was so sick and tired of the turmoil in me that I did not want to have anything to do with God or worship.

Then I began to read about revolutionaries who had toiled to eradicate this type of inequality in our society. The more I studied their principles and their way of life, the more I felt a deep sense of purpose, of peace. I felt an admiration, a reverence towards these honourable people. Also, I began to understand that men had created the indignity of the caste system and untouchability to suit their ends. I felt contempt for the Hindu religion, its gods and its sacred days. I heartily accepted the truth in what the rationalist Periyar Ramaswamy preached, 'The concept of God is created by the ignorant and the lazy. There is no God at all.'

Lord Buddha and Buddhism attracted me. Deciding not to remain in the Hindu religion with its unequal system of segregation, I visited mosques, churches and Buddhist temples. I read their holy books and appreciated the tenets of humaneness in them. But when I realized that people from every religion endured the same indignities; that there was no love or concern or respect between the privileged and the poor, I lost my fascination for any religion.

In 1980, I was appointed to the post of an attender in the First Grade College run by the Hyderabad Karnataka Education Society at Sadashivnagar. I was happy to move to the city. I believed that the stigma of caste would not hound me among city-bred, educated, enlightened and cultured people. My illusion was soon burnt to ashes.

The attender in the zoology department of the college P S Shivaprasadmurthy was a Lingayat. He showed off his caste with vibhoothi, the sacred ash generously smeared across his forehead, and with the Shivalinga dangling from his neck. I had heard that he had a book about the Buddha and I asked if I could borrow it. He said I could.

The two of us ate masala dosa and drank coffee at the Rajesh Hotel in Sadashivanagar. We chatted about this and that as we walked to his rented house in Gangenahalli. The clouds were in hiding, fearing the summer sun. Our heads were reeling under the heat and glare of the relentless sunshine. Our feet dragged on their own whenever we walked in the shade of trees. I bought a packet of peanuts for two rupees at Mekhri Circle. Murthy is greedy and exploitative; he grabbed handfuls and gobbled them up. As we neared his house, he ran ahead unexpectedly. He brought a wooden bench from inside, placed it outside the house and said, 'Sit here.' I felt it was below my dignity to sit on a bench outside his house. I walked away without saying anything; without taking the book.

Murthy's conscience would never tell him that it was not right to humiliate another person that way. A person with self-respect and self-worth would never disrespect another, would never look down on him. Shouldn't there be a reason for one to insult another? Someone who faces such humiliation can never ever forget it. Only a person who has been kicked feels the pain, not the one who kicked. Isn't that true? The memory of the humiliation seared my body and spirit. I felt like jaggery syrup in a cauldron, boiling and seething helplessly. Painful thoughts ravaged me, 'Why do these disgusting people ostracize me as if I were a leper the moment they get to know my caste?' I met a friend, got drunk with him and slept in that stupor.

When I woke up the next morning, the bitter memory of the humiliation plagued me. I compared Murthy and myself in terms of educational qualifications, job, intelligence, helping nature, sense of justice and right living, honesty and good behaviour. My conscience told me that I was in no way inferior to him.

Anjanappa was appointed as a sweeper in our college. He came to college all the way from Somanahalli near Kanakapura. He could not always afford to buy food; I helped him out with money at times. His relatives lived on this side of the city in Guttahalli. The elders of his family and that of a prospective bride arranged for a matrimonial alliance for him. When he had to visit the girl's family, he pleaded with me to go with him. I thought I would have no problems with the family, since Anjanappa was also a Dalit. I went along with him.

The girl's family served us lime juice. They were busy arranging for lunch. Anjanappa was stealing glances at the girl; she was stealing glances at him.

'Hunh, get up, get up. Come and wash your hands for lunch,' said the mother of the girl to us.

Anjanappa stared at me in the face! He stared at the lady too!

'Come and wash your hands. Lunch is ready,' she hurried us. Anjanappa signalled to her with his eyes. She blushed, bent her head and went to the inner rooms. The girl's father came out, carrying a chombu of water, and urged us, 'Come on! Wash your hands. It's getting late. Let's have lunch.'

Anajanappa signalled to him too. Both of them conversed with their hands and lips, as if they were deaf and dumb. Then, Anjanappa went outside and the host followed him. I got the message. I put on my socks and shoes and was tying my shoelaces.

'I won't have lunch, I'll come in the evening,' I heard Anjanappa whispering.

'Why? Why? What happened?' The man held Anjanappa's hands and pleaded. He looked flustered. Did it mean the boy did not approve of his daughter?

'Ayyo, don't worry!' said Anjanappa, 'The man sitting inside is a Madiga. That's why I don't want to eat now. I'll come alone this evening.'

The man cleared his throat loudly and spat. 'It's good for people to know their place,' he said, staring at me.

I felt as if a sword had pierced my heart. I was thrown off balance. I felt sweat streaming down my face. I was helpless with grief, with fury.

'Thu, it's better to commit suicide than to face insult from such people,' I decided. I did not eat anything the whole day.

That night, I sat watching the sky. That man's words bothered me, however much I tried to forget them. They kept eddying around me, targeting my spirit. My grief surfaced and I wept. I wept until I was exhausted, until I could weep no more. Thoughts of different forms of suicide floated in and out. Among them came a line from Dasa, the Vaishanava mendicant: *You have to swim; you have to live to win.* That gave me great comfort.

The tragedy in the story is that Anjanappa too is a Dalit like me; he is a Korama. Like me, he too was appointed to a post reserved for Dalits.

Of course, untouchables like us are cheated when people who are not untouchables are included in the scheduled caste categories for jobs. Posts reserved for us are given to them blatantly to benefit the government in power. We, who are smarting under the stigma of caste, continue to be exploited.

Gold was being beaten with an iron hammer in a goldsmith's house to shape it into ornaments. It submitted to the onslaught without a murmur. But a piece of iron, being similarly beaten to shape with an iron hammer at the iron monger's next door was screaming with pain. 'Ayyoyyo! Ayyoyyo!' When asked why, the gold bits said, 'Some others are beating me. So I suffer in silence.' And the piece of iron said, 'My own kind is pounding me. I'm sad. How can I keep quiet?'

There cannot be a more lamentable situation than Dalits demeaning Dalits.

Basavanna, a model social reformer, firmly believed that the devotees of Shiva were not bound by caste or the constraints of ritual purity and pollution. And to spread this belief, he performed the wedding of Lavanya, the daughter of the Brahmin Madhuvarasa with Sheelavantha, the son of Haralayya, a cobbler of the Maadhara community. But today, his Veershaiva followers are communalists on the one hand and fervent devotees of Shiva on the other. Basavanna will have to be born again to sort out this confusion.

But there are some who do follow his precepts faithfully.

I can never forget the goodness of Shrimathi Prathibhadevi Mudappa and her husband, Shri S B Mudappa, an IAS officer who was the chief secretary to the Government of Karnataka. She is the daughter of a former chief minister of Karnataka, S Nijalingappa. It is only because they are followers of Basavanna that they have helped me, though they know I am from a low caste. They have shown me the respect and concern that one person should show another. They do not reckon with the caste to which a person belongs, but with his character.

I was a member of the HKES Employees Co-operative Society. I was sanctioned a loan of five hundred rupees. Shrimathi Prathibhadevi Muddappa was the president of the

Society and I needed her signature on the cheque. P S S Murthy and I went to her house. I had previously decided that I would never ever cross the threshold of the houses of people who think they belong to a high caste, not for any reason whatever the circumstances.

'Ei, Murthy,' I said to my companion as we neared her house, 'Get Madam's signature on this cheque. I've got to see to something else.' I told him a lie.

'This cheque is yours. You get her to sign it now if you want. Or else, you can get it done when she comes to college.' Murthy walked away without even waiting for my reply.

I needed the money badly. But I could not handle the fear and anxiety raging through me: 'What new humiliations will I have to face if I enter the house?' I begged Murthy to get her signature. I promised to buy him delicious masala dosa, I cajoled him and sent him in. I stood at the gate.

I think Madam got to know about me standing at the gate.

'Come, Lachmana. Madam wants you,' Murthy called out.

'No, I won't. I promise I'll get you masala dosa. Please get her signature for me,' I pleaded with him.

At that very moment, Madam came out and called out to me, 'Barayya, ba. Come, come inside.' She knew very well that I was of a low caste. My legs began to tremble.

Decorated dolls had been arranged in the hall to celebrate Krishna Jayanthi, the birth of Krishna.

'Look at the dolls!' she said. She served me coffee. I sat trembling, curled up uncomfortably in fear. I could feel my heartbeat.

'Sit comfortably, Ayya,' Madam said.

'Truly, she is a Shivasharanaru, a follower of Shiva,' I said to myself.

Once, there was an occasion when I had to go to the house of Shri Mahadevappa Saathenahalli, a Kannada lecturer in our college. I got the address and located his house on Triveni Road.

Without his shirt, he looked quite portly. His forehead and hands were smeared with vibhoothi, the sacred ash. On his neck was a necklace of rudraksh beads. In his hand were agarbattis, scented sticks. He was doing his puja. As soon as he saw me, he stopped midway, held me by the hand, took me inside and made me sit on a bed. He treated me as a guest, serving me freshly made corn rotis, two types of vegetables, curds and rice followed by tea. My eyes filled.

Shri Mahadevappa Saathenahalli and I had often talked about the caste system and Basavanna's efforts to eradicate it through his followers, the Shiva Sharanas.

'Wear the Shivalinga and become a Lingayat,' he had advised me.

'Saar, I don't rob anyone, I don't kill, I don't tell lies. I do my duty diligently. My heart is pure. So, I don't need to wear the linga for show, do I? Do you really think this society will treat me with respect just because I dangle a Shivalinga from my neck?'

Shri Mahadevappa Saathenahalli was struck dumb. Only when such pure minds as his become the torrential rain from heaven will the flowers of equality bloom on earth. Plants, animals and birds are different in form and colour. But among people, the form, mind and heart are the same. And so, should there be a caste difference among us?

Don't say, Madiga, Madiga,
Holeya...Madiga, Swami.
Holeyas and Madigas too

Are people, Mahaswami.
They wake up at cock-crow.
They clean up the village and the slum.
They eat their hunger and wear their shame,
And live on the outskirts,
These Holeyas and Madigas.
They eat dead cows and buffaloes
They cobbler slippers and shoes
They carry the dead
And dream of water and shelter,
These Holeyas and Madigas.
Their hands and legs, nose and ears
Hearts and minds, tongue and eyes
Are no different from anyone else's
How come then that they pollute?
Pain and joy and sorrow
Are the same for one and all.
Where's the need for difference?
For high and low in humankind?
When all have birth and death, pain and joy,
Flesh and blood and the pulse in the blood?
If you call us Holeya, Madiga,
I may touch your feet in respect
Or else I may….

The Craze for an Education Society

On the first of August every year, the staff of the HKES Society celebrated the birthday of the late founder Shri Mahadevappa Rampure with much pomp and splendour, remembering him with gratitude and sharing sweetmeats in his name. On that occasion, a few speakers spoke about the force of Shri Rampure's personality and vision in establishing and guiding the society to its present stature. A holiday was declared for the college.

And then, on the second of June every year, the society commemorated his death anniversary. On that occasion, some of the staff members grieved as if they had lost a family member. They spoke of the gratitude we owe him; we were eating the fruit of his labour, we had our jobs because of his society.

I realized the stupendous truth that, thanks to Shri Mahadevappa Rampure's endeavour, thousands of families thrived, thousands upon thousands of students were educated and I had a job.

A new sense of purpose took hold of me, goading me day and night towards an indistinct goal: Once a man is born, he has to die. But his death should be worthwhile. Though he dies, his name should be evergreen on the earth. Thousands of people should remember him. I should live for such a desire. My life should benefit others.

I learnt about Shri Rampure from those who knew him personally. Once, when I was in the library, a booklet entitled *Mahadevapparampure* caught my eye. My curiosity about the man increased and I sat down to read it. I was so engrossed in it that I forgot to have my lunch. Here are a few excerpts from that booklet:

When Rampure's grandfather looked up to see how tall his grandson had grown, his cap fell to the floor.

When Rampure died, the whole of Kalburgi was slushy with the tears of the mourners.

These words of Shri Biraadhar impressed me. A desire that I too should start an education society sprouted in me. I shared it with many of my friends.

'Your idea is good, no doubt,' some said. 'But, after all, we're Dalits. It's not that easy to set up an educational society. You need land, funds and government support.'

'Why do you have such big dreams at such a young age?' said some others, 'Why don't you eat and drink and enjoy life instead?'

And yet, the desire to set up an education society would not let go of me.

One day, while having coffee at Kamat Hotel on J C Road with my friends L Hanumanthaiah and M C K Murthy, I told them of my desire.

'Is that ever possible?' said L Hanumanthaiah, 'Is it child's play to set up an education society, Lakshman? Such things are only for those who have inherited a fortune or for politicians. Don't put your hand to it. Don't ruin your peace of mind. Don't ruin ours as well. We're not going to put up your statue if you start an education society.'

M C K Murthy, young as he was, started off on the benefits of running such a society in terms of standing, of monetary gain…he let drive a speech for about half an hour. The young man was running a small-scale industry. He always had money in hand. He was a smart guy with a car.

'I'll take up the financial responsibility,' he said. 'You see to the registration and other things from tomorrow.'

L Hanumanthaiah needed the help of moneyed friends every evening. Perhaps, because of that predicament, he too changed his stand.

'Fine, let's get the society registered tomorrow,' he said and added, 'Hanh, if we have to think through such earth-shaking matters, we need a bottle or two of beer to chill our bellies, don't we?' His artificial grin displayed all his broken teeth. M C K Murthy got us beer at Hotel Select.

The list of members of the society was ready the very next day.

The poet, Siddalingaiah – President

M C K Murthy – Vice-president

L Hanumanthaiah – Secretary

Lakshman (I) – Treasurer

Mohan Kumar – Member

Dayanathan – Member

Kanteerava Pragathi Education Society was registered.

In 1985, we submitted a petition to the government for permission to start the Pragathi Education Society Pre-University College. Shri Kantharaj, Superintendent, Department of Pre-

University Education helped us a great deal. At that time, the poet Siddalingaiah was a member of the Pre-University Board. Since he was also the president of the society, we hoped to get the approval for the college without any trouble.

C Muniraju of Kanteeravanagar took Rs 18,000/- to construct the college and left us in the lurch midway. I begged and pleaded with N K Chandrashekar, a student at the HKES College, and procured bricks on credit. I drew water by pumping a borewell near a swamp from six in the evening to ten at night every day. Shri K P Thimmarayappa walked back and forth carrying the water to the construction site in two metal pots. Toiling thus day and night, we were able to build five rooms for the college. I was able to get chairs, tables and cupboards on credit from a showroom belonging to Ashwinikumar, a student of HKES College.

In June, Pragathi Pre-University College of the Pragathi Education Society was open for admissions, but not many students applied. We went out with handbills to Kolar district and brought back Dalit students. We even opened a hostel for them. Both the college and the hostel flourished. I gained a new kind of respect. I was so happy to see my dream come true that I slogged for the college day and night, forgetting wife and children, home and the Dalit Sangarsha Samiti.

Shri Ramakrishna Hegde was the chief minister of Karnataka at that time. His cabinet declared that permission would not be granted for new colleges for five years from the current year. Our college had been running for three months by then. What would be the future of our students? The parents of the children would not take this lightly. What was I to do? I was worried.

'Let's transfer our students to Nolamba Pre-University College,' suggested the poet Siddalingaiah. 'And let's pay back all the expenses we've incurred for the college and the society and bid goodbye to the project bringing our palms together with due respect.'

Baraguru Ramachandrappa, a Bandaya writer of repute, heard about our predicament.

'Let's talk to the chief minister once,' he said. But we had to get an appointment to meet the chief minister and no one was willing to take that step.

I requested Shrimathi Prathibhadevi Muddappa, a lecturer in Zoology, HKES College, to get me an appointment with the chief minister. That compassionate lady called up her husband, S B Mudappa. He called up the chief minister's PA and fixed up an interview with him at ten minutes to ten o'clock in the morning at his office at Krishna.

I informed Baraguru Ramachandrappa and the members of the Society.

On that day, the poet Siddalingaiah, L Hanumanthaiah, MCK Murthy and I waited at Krishna for the chief minister. Shri Ramakrishna Hegde arrived. We greeted him bringing our palms together. Shri Hegde hugged Siddalingaiah.

'How're you, Siddalingaiah? What did you want of me?' he asked.

The poet narrated the story about us starting the college and our present predicament in a touching manner. He explained that we needed the chief minister's sanction for us to continue. Immediately, the chief minister took our petition and signed on it. From that moment, I floated in a sea of inexpressible peace, happiness and fulfillment.

Once I was able to get fifty kgs of rice free for the hostel, thanks to the benevolence of Hunumantharayappa of Kamalanagar in Rajajinagar. It was around ten at night when

I left Kamalanagar on my Hero Majestic, a two-wheeler. The front wheel had a flat tyre when I neared Shankar Mutt. How could I leave the vehicle anywhere? Or the bag of half a quintal of rice? The hostel was about three kilometres away.

As I was pushing the bike uphill with the heavy load, I got a catch on my right side. I could neither sit nor stand; I felt I was dying. I struggled like a fish out of water. I breathed through my mouth and my nose. My throat was dry; I had no saliva in my mouth. I stood awhile. I felt better. A thought came to me in the cool breeze as it were, 'Remove the chain from the moped. You'll be able to push it easily.' Immediately, I tugged at the chain. Sarak! It snapped. I was able to push it smoothly along the level road. But the uphill climbs were dreadful. My thighs trembled with the strain. I felt as if my gut had come to my mouth.

I got the rice cooked at K P Thimmaiah's house and some tomato chutney to go with it. I woke up the starving hostelites and had dinner with them. Then I went home. My wife was sitting by the light of the kerosene lamp, worried. Debtors had plagued her the whole day through; those who had supplied firewood and groceries on credit to the hostel, the newspaper agent…They had come all the way from Bayaagna to demand their dues; they had abused her. She wept as she told me all this.

They would come again the next morning; they would scold us again. I did not want the sun to rise, ever. I could not sleep. I wrote the first story in my life: *Why does day break at all?*

It was quite some time before the society discovered that L Hanumanthaiah had taken money in the name of the society from the college staff, and that he had also misappropriated the scholarship money meant for the Dalit students.

'All of us belong to the Dalit Movement. We're fighting in our limited ways against injustice. We're hurt to find such injustice and exploitation within our own society. Kindly return the money you've taken. This is a matter concerning the name of the society. Please don't ruin it.' All of us pleaded with him, trusting in our fellow-feeling for one another. He had swindled more than a lakh in the name of the society. He did not care for our words of intimate friendship. He had already dug several pits in which to throw us.

First, that cheat tried to tarnish the name of Siddalingaiah. He had filled me with such stories about the poet that I did not want to look him in the face. For whatever his reason, Siddaligaiah resigned from the society. Mohan Kumar and Dayanathan began to fear the very shadow of L Hanumanthaiah. M C K Murthy had been the first person to invest in the society. L Hanumanthaiah began to spread a rumour that he was involved in misappropriation of funds. There was some truth in it, of course. Even as Murthy was trying to sort it out with us, he met with an accident on his scooter and fractured his leg. He did not come anywhere near the college. He could not walk for almost a year.

I was saddened that the society I had built with hundreds of dreams had cheated the public. No one came forward to help me repay the debts incurred in running the college.

Today, if I read or see or hear about any confidence trickster in any movie, book, news item or conversation, I think of L Hanumanthaiah. *A smooth talker can survive even during famine* is a familiar proverb. L Hanumanthaiah was such a conman; we were stupid. Just as foxes let down the tip of their tails into canals to catch a meal of crabs effortlessly, even so L Hanumanthaiah ate up every founder member of the society, drank water and belched.

I will never forget the hunger, loss and disgrace I suffered for the sake of the society. There is something else that is worse;

I have become suspicious of people in general. Even when someone talks about his troubles and losses, I doubt the truth of what he is saying before I accept it. And it is Hanumanthaiah who has changed my trustful mindset.

It is impossible to set up and run an Education Society among people who have no sense of accountability. It has to be the work of honest, like-minded people. Or else, the project becomes a white elephant. We have to take donations from the students. That is a kind of exploitation. True. There is no scope for humaneness or social concern here. It is much like in private hospitals where the families have to pay up the dues to take the body of their dear ones, even if they cannot afford to. The owner may feel rotten to insist on the payment, but he cannot help it if he wants to run his hospital effectively. So it is with education. Anyway, L Hanumanthaiah cured me of that craze for an Education Society.

For Which Mansion Are You the Foundation Stones?

Those were the early days of the Karnataka Vimochana Ranga, the Karnataka Liberation Front. Jayaprakash met me every three days, or at least once a week. He talked about the inevitability of a national struggle. As in the proverb: *Even the string that holds the flowers in a strand offered to god goes to heaven with them*, I too joined the Ranga, a forum born out of the hard work and perseverance of my companions. I became one of the founder members. Initially, I was the joint-secretary for the state. Later, I experienced the joys and sorrows of being the vice president at the national level.

My friends were like oil lamps, burning their wicks to bring light to others. They lived frugally. They were self-reflexive, dreaming of a nation built on equality. They were as silent as the skies. True. But they could also speak like the roaring wave of the sea about ways of realizing their dreams. With hearts as innocent as a child's, they smiled through their difficulties like the gurgling river. They believed they had inherited the whole world and were responsible for it; not only for their parents, relatives and friends, slum and village. They had burnt to ashes the natural desire for personal security and happiness. They forgot hunger, thirst and sleep.

I had learnt the hard way that everything that is white is not butter; I had learnt to see the difference between butter and quicklime. And so, I was in the police records as a revolutionary. I was suspect.

Once, the national-level general body meeting of the Ranga was at Mutthiguntte in Kohlar district. We reached the village at four in the evening. We had not eaten the whole day; we did not have any money, anyway. There were only three plates in the house where the meeting was to be held. The hosts offered one each to Prof. Ramalingam and Shrirangacharya. Jayaprakash and I ate from the third plate. The meal was broken-rice gruel with greens curry. That was the first time in my life that I had eaten with a non-Dalit from the same plate.

Some of the factories set up in the Kolhar Industrial Area in Bidar District were polluting the environment. The national committee of the Ranga held lengthy discussions in the sylvan surroundings of Shringeri on the injustice the Dalits and the villagers in the locality had to endure due to the damage to life and property.

After the national-level conference at Shringeri, we were heading back to Bangalore at ten that night in a private bus run by Balaji Transport. It was around three in the morning when we were crossing the peaceful forest near Thirthahalli. Everyone except the driver was in blissful sleep. A tame elephant dragging a heavy chain tied to its leg was walking with a wild one. The driver stopped the bus as soon as he saw them and turned off the lights. The tame elephant crossed the road and disappeared into the forest. The wild elephant too crossed the road and stepped towards the edge of the forest, but then, turned back for no reason at all. It came to the bus and lashed it once with its trunk. The windscreen splintered. It trumpeted once. Our sleep dashed into the forest, leaving us wide awake. The elephant bashed its head against the bus in fury. Its tusks got caught in the windows. As it swayed to free them, the bus swayed with it. The passengers were crying out in fear for their lives.

'Please don't make any noise. Please don't cry. The elephant will topple the bus in its fury,' whispered the conductor, walking down the aisle and pacifying them.

The trumpeting of the elephant and the swaying of the bus may have gone on for about three to four minutes. We had lost all hopes of surviving the ordeal when, suddenly, the elephant extricated its tusks from the bus and ambled away into the jungle, even as we watched it stupefied. The bus had no lights now, but the driver drove it carefully through the forest all the way to Shivamogga.

The electrical wiring was repaired in Shivamogga and the bus began to move, even while the driver was still lying under the bus. With great presence of mind, the conductor put a log near the front wheel to stop it. When they checked the bus again, they found a flat tire—the tube had burst. Once they changed the tire, the bus went smoothly. But we were not at peace until we reached Bengaluru.

'Che…What a waste of life if we had died this way!' said Shri Shivalingam, 'Our death should have a meaning.'

The people in the villages around Kolhar in Bidar district faced a lot of problems to get drinking water. Their cattle died after drinking water from ponds and tanks. Poisonous snakes were found dead everywhere. The people had strange diseases like elephantiasis. Pregnant women began to bleed. Sugarcane grew in abundance, but the jaggery made from its juice was as black as tar. Though there were countless problems arising out of environmental pollution in the area, none of the vote-seeking political parties had tackled them. They were blind, though they could see because they were subservient to a financier in Andhra Pradesh and imperialistic powers like Europe and America.

The Ranga organized many protests against the situation. But the condition remained the same. Our Dalit fellowmen and farmers did not get justice. Frustrated agitators set fire to the warehouse of the Sole Company in Bengaluru. The police could not ferret out the agitators involved, and so they filed a case against all the members in the Sangha. Sirimane Nagaraj, Parvatheesh, Banjagere and Jayaprakash entered the Central Jail in Bengaluru. Shivalingam and I went underground for two weeks until we could get anticipatory bail. C H Hanumantharaya took up our case without any payment because we were revolutionaries.

During the fifteen days that I was in hiding, Shri Basavaraj Kouthal, a Dalit activist, helped me in every way possible.

'Your field of action is the literary field,' he advised me repeatedly, 'You have to be an asset to the members of the organization through your writings. Also, it is imperative for every member to save his skin.'

The case dragged on in the court unnecessarily for four years. Finally, the verdict was in our favour; all of us were cleared.

One thing that has always intrigued me is the spartan existence of my companions in the Karnataka Vimochana Ranga. They wear hand-me-down clothes and slippers and work for the liberation of the downtrodden. They eat if they are given something, or else they go hungry. What should we call such people who have triumphed over hunger and thirst? I do not know. I respect the philosophy and precepts that steer the Ranga by supporting my fellow workers in their nationwide struggle with heartfelt love and regard.

One of my co-workers M C Krishna met me often to discuss relevant issues. For about two years, I had seen him wearing the same sweater. It was thick enough to make him perspire even in winter. I heard that he organized student units. I could not bear to see him in that pullover, and so I bought a shirt-length for him.

'Please get this stitched,' I said, handing him the shirt material and fifty rupees as tailoring charges.

He looked stunned. He would not accept it.

'You get it stitched for yourself,' he said, 'It'll look good on you.'

'This is my gift of affection for you. Reject it if you wish to.'

'Saar, please don't take me amiss. I wore new clothes until I was eight years old. Around that time, I got to know about this organization. Since then I haven't worn anything new, nor will I ever do,' he said stiffly like snapping a dry twig.

'If you reject this, you're treating my friendship with contempt. Do you realize that?' I scolded him.

He thought for a moment and stuffed the shirt-length into his shoulder bag. Though we did meet several times after that, the sweater had not made way for the shirt. Somehow, we lost the camaraderie we shared. I hear he is married. He is working for some newspaper as a reporter. He got me coffee with the same old warmth when we met on some occasion recently.

Countless young men like him are seeds sown for a rich harvest of a nation of humane citizens. They sacrifice the good things of life; they sacrifice life itself in their fight for a just and equitable society that looks upon all people as equal. Their labour will not be in vain; it will be worthwhile.

People like them all across the world have built healthier societies in some countries; are aspiring to build healthy societies in some others.

Some of us like-minded people have started the Jaathi Vinaashaka Vedhike. It is a forum for the eradication of caste. This organization has brought fresh hopes and desires to people of all castes and classes. It has begun its activities in a few districts in the state. The responsibilities of the founder president of this organization too rest on my shoulders. Whatever be my limitations, I will toil for the eradication of the caste system.

May casteism perish!

May humaneness thrive!

Praise to Our Ancestors–An Afterword

As I grew older, I recalled my childhood experiences and learnt to see them with new eyes.

I relived the time the rains came when we had placated Maleraaya. The Gowda community in our village had worshiped the Rain God for eleven days, carrying him from house to house for water to be poured over him as hymns were sung. And yet, not a single drop of rain quenched the parched earth. The elders of the village got together and discussed among themselves, 'Madigas belong to the ancestry of Jambavantha. They are people of integrity like him. Won't Maleraaya come down if they invite him?' And so they asked us to do the ritual to appease Maleraaya. We stood in front of the home of every Gowda. They poured water over the idol of Maleraaya that we carried, smeared it with a pinch of kumkum and arshna and lit a scented stick or two in worship and sent us on after honouring us as the ritual required. And the rains came in torrents by the third day. It was only because I had been born a Madiga that the Gowdas respected me that day. They worshipped us as children of the Madiga community, speaking to us kindly and treating us as special. This incident made a great impact on me as I understood its significance. I became interested in getting to know about my ancestors.

We trace our ancestry to Jambavantha of mythic times. He was a famous general in Sugreeva's army that fought for Rama against Ravana. He was also a sage as per the Marulasiddhantha. Medieval writings record Maadhara Chennaya, Dhoolayya and Kallavva who composed vachanas as people of great repute.

We must note here that the mystic Ravidasa of North India belonged to the Chammara community. As per the tradition of his time, he worked as a cobbler like his forefathers. But he skinned and tanned only the skin of carcasses; he never killed animals. People of the upper castes respected him for this. He spent his life singing Hari's praises. He spent all his earnings on mass-feeding sadhus. After he left his father's home, his financial situation became lamentable; he could hardly afford a daily meal. God himself grieved at his condition and appeared in the form of a sadhu at Ravidasa's doorstep. Ravidasa welcomed the monk with great joy and devotion. God was so pleased with Ravidasa's hospitality that he offered him a philosopher's stone telling him that it could turn base metals into gold. But Ravidasa did not want the stone. He was living like an ascetic, having renounced his worldly wealth.

'Bring me something made of metal,' said God, thinking he might be tempted if he saw gold. Except for an idol, everything else in the house was made of clay. Then God spotted the cobbler's awl and touched it with the stone. Immediately, the awl sparkled, thalathala. Looking at his awl, Ravidasa was more sad than happy. He was shrouded with fear that he would not be able to use his awl, his sole means of livelihood.

'Please turn the awl back to iron, mahaswami,' pleaded Ravidasa. 'I'm quite happy making an honest living with it. I'm blessed enough to feed sadhus like you with my meagre earnings. I won't know how to handle the wealth that may come my way with the stone.'

God changed the awl to iron and once again asked Ravidasa to accept the stone. He would not. God, then, wrapped it in a rag and stuck it between some coconut fronds in the thatched hut and told him to use it in case of necessity. A year later, God appeared again to Ravidasa in the guise of the same sadhu.

'Was the stone useful in anyway?' he asked.

Ramadasa had quite forgotten about it. He had been engrossed in meditating on Hari and feeding sadhus. God took the stone from where he had placed it and went away, pleased with Ravidasa's devotion.

Such great people accomplishing such great spiritual feats were our ancestors. The gorava, jogathi and aasaadhi traditions of Mylaralinga in practice to this day are proof of our spiritual outlook. In a way, we too have been influenced by their sense of detachment; we are tenacious in our struggle for justice, even though we know we might not always win.

In 1992, Shri Ramaswami Shivaacharya suggested that the expression Madiga could be a derivation of 'the people of Mahadeva': Mahadevaru -> Maadevaru -> Maadaru -> Madigaru.

There is a legend about how we became a tanner-cobbler community:

One hot summer's day, our ancestors Haralayya and Kalyanamma met Basavanna on the way.

'Sharanu, Swami,' said Haralayya.

'Sharanu sharanaarthi,' responded Basavanna. Haralayya was touched that Basavanna greeted him twice over, though he was of a low caste. So he and his wife peeled the skin off their thighs and made him a pair of slippers.

'These should belong to Kudala Sangama Deva,' said Basavanna, placing the slippers on his head.

This is the heritage of our community, and to this we shall strive to be true as far as we can. Despite the indignities we have suffered down the ages, there have been seasons of respite during seasons of revival; whenever the Buddhist spirit of compassion was strong in Karnataka, whenever tolerance was furthered by the Sharanas. Their mindset has boosted our resolve to fight for justice as our moral duty. I have slogged in the Dalit Sangarsha Samiti for forty years, taking part in countless protests against discrimination, injustice and murder. I am currently involved in the Jaathi Vinaashaka Vedige. I hope to strive for the eradication of caste as long as I have life in me. Our social standing as a community may not have changed much, but we have definitely gained a sense of self-worth and, with it, a sense of purpose.

But ironically, our purpose also seems to be to victimize our own people. We are now facing new kinds of discrimination from within.

Twenty kilometres from Bengaluru city, there is a temple of Rudhreshwara in Jayanagara, Nelamangala Taluk. Two years ago, nine-year-old Navin and eight-year-old Santosh stretched out their hands in hunger when the purohit distributed prasad.

'Which caste?' asked the purohit, looking at their clothes.

'Madigas.'

The purohit kicked Navin. He fell down, jumped up and ran away. The purohit caught hold of Santosh and bashed his head against the wall until the boy was drenched in blood. He was taken to the Government Hospital in Nelamangala for treatment. He needed eight sutures. Members of Jaathi Vinaashaka Vedhike and Dalit Sangarsha Samiti protested against the heinous act and saw to it that the purohit was imprisoned. But the purohit got a false certificate to say that he was a Dalit and pleaded his case in court. He was released. He disappeared. Dalit or not, wasn't the purohit guilty? Should he not be punished?

Barely four months ago, Abhishek, a Madiga boy from Babu Jagjeevanramnagar in Gubbi, Tumkur, was in love with Padmavathi of the Thigalara caste. Her father Kaadu Prakash abducted Abhishek, stripped him that in a graveyard, garlanded him with slippers and told him that was the punishment for being in love with his daughter. Not just that. He got a few people to beat up the boy, leaving him half dead. Was he right?

People of the upper castes do not exploit us only out of contempt or prejudice. They do it for convenience too.

There is a legend about a village called Eradukere on the Karnataka border with Andhra Pradesh. Marigowda, a Vokkaliga, struggled for three years to build a tank, with the Madigas providing free labour. But the tank-bund gave way with the onset of every monsoon season. And it kept collapsing, though it was rebuilt with stronger reinforcements about four times. Marigowda was worried; he had lost much in terms of money and labour. How would he explain to those who had provided technical expertise and financial help? He gave up food and drink. He became ill with anxiety.

One night, Gangadevi appeared to him in his dream. Marigowda felt that he heard her say, 'The bank will stand only if you sacrifice your pregnant daughter-in-law to me.' He sat up with a start. He felt the sky had fallen on him. Everyone who heard about his dream was upset too; his wife, relatives and the elders of the village. The only daughter-in-law, pregnant with her first child, the fond wife of his only son! The beautiful daughter of a wealthy, reputed family! No one wanted food or drink. Where could they find sleep and rest then? The house was like a graveyard.

The shanboga of the village was Marigowda's close friend.

'Stop losing sleep over this,' he said, 'Isn't your bonded labourer Budhiga's son Thimmaga like a son to you? Isn't his wife, Bandhamma, a daughter-in-law then? She too is pregnant. You could sacrifice her, can't you?'

Following that advice, the Gowda's family adorned Bandhamma with a new sari and jewellery. They decked her with flowers and smeared her with the sacred arshna-kumkum. They took her in procession towards the tank-bund accompanied by loud music. A great throng followed them. They reached the area where the bund had given way. Faint weeping was heard despite the loud music renting the air. Bandhamma's new sari and jewels were removed. She was forced to sit in a pit that was then covered with a stone slab. Heavy monsoon rains lashed the village after Bandhamma was buried alive. But the banks of the tank held firm. Bandamma became a goddess in everyone's sight. Marigowda erected a small temple with a few slabs of stone. He installed a wooden doll in it to represent Bandhamma. From then onwards, both Marigowda's family and Bandhamma's husband's family worshipped her in that temple on sacred days. Marigowda and a few other landowners gifted to Bandamma's husband's family two acres of land near the graveyard beyond the tank.

To this day, Tippegowda, Shankaragowda and Marigowda who belong to that elder Marigowda's family worship at Bandhamma's temple before any auspicious occasion. Every year on Chandramana Yugaadhi, Marigowda's progeny celebrate the New Year by offering to Bandhamma's progeny the ritual gifts given to a married woman—a new sari, blouse, bangles, fruits, coconut, flowers, kumkum, arshna—together with a bull. They, in return, receive the gifts with deep gratitude and worship their ancestor Bandhamma.

There was a similar situation last year. Basavaraju, a seventeen-year-old Madiga from Thirumalakoppa village in Ranibennuru, was bound hand and foot. After a puja, a nail was driven into his head and blood was collected and sprinkled inside a house. His body was thrown behind the house. His mouth was stuffed with cotton. He had been given a medicine with alcohol that makes a person unconscious. Reason? The house belonging to an upper-caste was not vaastu-compliant; it needed human sacrifice to become habitable. And so Basavaraju was killed to rectify its dosha. Our friends Shivalingamma and Santhali wrote to certain people. As a result, the guilty person was jailed.

Though there are laws to protect us, though we are vigilant enough to raise a hue and cry when they fail, atrocities against Dalits do carry on.

You are a light unto yourself, said Buddha. All those who are exploited must feel it their responsibility to stand up against exploitation without compromise. Only then can we stand with our heads held high. Only then can light shine in every home.

We may not always be successful, but fight we must.

Glossary

Aasaadhi	:	cobbler community
akshathe	:	grains of rice sanctified with turmeric for auspicious occasions
Ambedkar	:	social reformer from Maharashtra, inspired the Dalit Buddhist Movement to support the rights of the Dalits
arshna	:	turmeric
Basavanna	:	social reformer from Karnataka, a mystic of the twelfth century who moved away from the Vedic priestly tradition and founded the Lingayat faith
Bhavabhuthi	:	scholar of the eighth century, noted for his plays
Bhuthaayi	:	Mother Earth
chombu	:	a metal pot
Deepavali	:	Festival of Lights
devara konda	:	a fire-walking ceremony where devotees walk across a pit filled with embers
dosha	:	defect
ede	:	food offered to the dead on festive days
ganji	:	gruel
Goravas	:	members of the Kuruba community of shepherds. Their leader Mylara fought against the demon, Mallaasura; Shaivite mendicants
gundas	:	trouble-makers
hittukolu	:	a wooden stick used to stir ragi flour in hot water to make ragi balls
Holeya	:	member of a community that once cleaned dry toilets; Holeya (singular), Holeyaru (plural) Holathi (feminine)

Jangama	:	a wandering mystic from the Vaishnava sect
jogathis	:	ascetic women
kalasa, kalasha	:	a metal pot with water, topped with mango leaves and a coconut, used in Hindu rituals
karawada thanni	:	illicit liquor
Kudala Sangama Deva	:	the deity of a place of pilgrimage in Karnataka where Krishna and Malaprabha rivers merge and flow towards Srisaila in Andhra Pradesh
kumkum	:	a sanctified red powder that Hindus wear as a dot between the eye brows
Madiga	:	a cobbler or tanner or, in contemporary life, the pourakarmika or sweeper
Mahanavami, Marnomi	:	the ninth day of the Dasara festivities
mahaswami	:	an address of deep respect
mangalaarathi	:	the ritual of waving a lamp in front of a deity
Maramma	:	folk deity representing the feminine energy
masaladosai	:	a savoury snack; a speciality in Karnataka
mettukolu	:	a V-shaped wooden stick used to hold the pot in place while stirring ragi flour in hot water to make ragi balls
mudhuka	:	old man
mudhuki	:	old woman
Mylaralinga	:	a form of Shiva in Mylara, Karnataka
Navagrahas	:	the nine planets
Periyar Ramaswamy	:	social reformer from Tamil Nadu, founded the Self-Respect Movement to eradicate the caste system
prasad	:	a portion of the offering to the idol returned to the worshipper as a blessing
puja	:	worship
purohit	:	temple-priest

rangoli	:	decorative designs drawn on the floor with a white powder or paste
Ravana	:	the king of Lanka who abducts Rama's wife Sita in the epic Ramayana
rudhrakshi	:	a berry sacred to Shiva
saar	:	an Indian version of Sir
saadhu	:	a dot of a black resin that Madigas put as caste-mark between the eyebrows
shanboga	:	village accountant
thambula	:	betel leaves and areca nuts offered on auspicious occasions
thamte	:	a kind of drum
thavarumane	:	mother's house
thoti	:	scavenger
Tigalaru	:	a Tamilian Dalit community in Karnataka
Sharanas	:	worshippers of Shiva
Shivalinga, linga	:	symbol of Shiva's creative energy in the form of a phallus
upaadhane	:	the ritual of receiving alms
vachanas	:	poetic prose compositions by Virashaiva mystics of the twelfth century
vaasthu	:	traditional Hindu system of architecture
vibhoothi	:	sacred ash; Shaivites smear it on the body
Vokkaliga	:	a dominant caste in Karnataka; an agricultural community
Yugaadhi	:	Lunar New Year's Day

Note on the Author

Lakshman (1957–2017) was from Kathriguppe, a village in South Bengaluru Taluk. His parents Muthappa and Venkatamma were daily-wage labourers. He studied in the Government Primary School in Kathruguppe and the Government Boys Middle School in Basavanagudi and completed his studies at the Government Fort High School, Chamarajapet, residing at the Shri Narasimharaja Hostel, Chamarajapet. He was a second division clerk at HKED Veerendra Patil Pre-University College since 1980.

As a social activist, he served as general secretary, Karnataka Dalit Sangarsha Samiti, founder member and national vice president of Karnataka Vimochana Ranga and founder president of Jaathi Vinaashaka Vedhike.

As a writer, he has many collections of poems, short stories and two novels to his credit. The novels *Jadimale* and *Badhuku* have been translated into Tamil. Some of the awards he has received are: Rashtrakavi Kuvempu Award (2003), Dr Ambedkar Fellowship National Award (2006) and Karnataka Keerthi Kalasa State Award (2007).

Note on the Translator

Susheela Punitha has translated from Kannada to English, excerpts on theatre in Karnataka for *Regional Theatre Histories*, Institute of Economic Growth, University of Delhi Enclave, Delhi, and the following works of fiction for Oxford University Press: *Hundreds of Streets to the Palace of Lights and Other Stories*, a collection of short stories by S Diwakar (2015), *Dweepa*, a novella by Na. D'Souza (2013), *Asprushyaru*, a novel by Vaidehi, as *Vasudeva's Family* (2012) and *Bharathipura*, a novel by U R Ananthamurthy (2010).

Bharathipura was shortlisted for the Jaipur Literary Prize, 2012 and The Hindu Literary Prize, 2012. *Hundreds of Streets to the Palace of Lights* was shortlisted for the Crossword Book Award, 2016.

Susheela Punitha received the Sahitya Akademi Translation Award for English, 2015, for her translation of U R Ananthamurthy's novel *Bharathipura*.

Note on the Writer of the Introduction

Dr V S Sreedhara taught English at Vijaya and St Joseph's Colleges in Bangalore, before he moved to the National Law School of India University where he was an assistant professor and deputy director of the Centre for the Study of Social Exclusion and Inclusive Policy. He is also with Human Rights group 'Peoples' Democratic Forum'.